Outline of the Epistle of Paul to the Ephesians

Volume 26

———⬧⬥⬧———

CHARLES A. COATES
1862 - 1945

Scripture references are generally from the King James Bibles unless otherwise noted.

* * * * *

Page numbering does not correspond to the published Index of C.A.C's ministry. This because this volumea contains larger type and larger page sizes, which affect the pagination.

This edition is published by:

BIBLES, etc.

www.bibles-etc.com

ISBN: 978-0-912868-31-8

Available from:
www.LuLu.com

Biography of Charles Andrew Coates

This book is part of a large series from original sources of published ministry given over many years by Charles A Coates, who was born in Bradford, England, in December 1862, and died in Teignmouth, Devon in October 1945.

He relates that he started writing and publishing tracts at the age of 22, and by 1900, books collecting his lectures and writings began a limited private circulation. Interest led to more general publication of several collections included in this series. His ministry is now widely appreciated and has been frequently republished. Mr Coates may be best known for a series of Outlines of many books of the Bible. These are later than the collected tracts and lectures, being based on notes of Bible readings from 1920 up until shortly before his death, almost all of which were revised by him. A lot more of his ministry has been published since his death.

Mr Coates' ministry reflects his long life of devoted service to the Lord, and the depth and extent of his love and appreciation of divine truth. It is valued for its clarity and accessibility, and many have been drawn into the study of the Word by starting with one or other of his books. He cuts in a straight line the word of truth; not only accurate in his interpretation, but also direct and faithful in the application of the truth to our walk and conduct. He is sound on the foundations of the gospel, giving extensive guidance and assurance to souls seeking establishment in their faith.

Walter Brown sums up Mr Coates in this introduction to his published letters -

> Our brother's active service was for many years much restricted through bodily weakness, and this contributed, under the Lord's hand, to the development of ... choice spiritual feelings. His mind was remarkably formed by the teaching of the Holy Scriptures, and all that he wrote was the result of prayerful consideration. Hence the combination of unswerving faithfulness to the Lord with true humility and gracious sympathy in the spiritual experiences of others. Above all else, the reader cannot fail

to remark in these pages our beloved brother's deep appreciation of the Person of Christ, and his wholehearted devotedness to His interests on earth, centring in "His body, which is the assembly". No matter affecting the Lord or His saints was regarded as too trivial for his interest and prayers, and the smallest service done for His Name and glory found recognition and appreciation.

Charles Coates was born and brought up in Yorkshire. His father, James Coates, was born in Scotland in 1809. James is said to have once been a shepherd, but from no later than 1841, he was a linen draper in Bradford. He was moved to withdraw from the Congregational Chapel there in 1846 to be among the brethren in the town; and in 1855 was married to Elizabeth Rollinson, born in nearby Otley in 1820.

Charles was converted at the age of 16 – a turning point he marked by writing the first of several hymns. Sometime before his mother died in 1905, he moved with her to Paignton, Devon. After she died, he had lodgings in Teignmouth, and lived and broke bread there until his death. He never married. Mr Coates started working with his father as a draper, but evidently gave this up -perhaps when his father died: his health was poor from an early age. His infirmity also limited how much he travelled, so that much of his ministry was either given locally, or written.

This set of books is published with the desire that others may find and get the benefit of what the Lord gave His people through our brother; and that this will be to God's glory.

D. Andrew Burr
February 2021

Contents

Reading 1 - *Probably at Teignmouth*
Ephesians 1:1-14

C.A.C. We have in this epistle the whole unfolding of what is for the divine pleasure. We all know that the epistles to the Romans and to the Ephesians are the two great presentations of positive truth: the one gives us the ministry of the gospel and the other the ministry of the assembly. The ministry of the gospel shows what there is for man and the ministry of the assembly shows what there is for divine Persons.

We get a setting forth here of what is for the divine pleasure; that company which is called to such peculiar privilege is the company of many sons which form the assembly. It is what God has proposed from all eternity; it has been a deliberate matter with God. The thought of choosing before the world's foundation implies the deliberate choice of God, His purpose and His counsel. The word 'counsel' implies deliberation, it is not a thing done on the spur of the moment. It was the profound consideration of the blessed God as to what He was about to do for His own pleasure; we get here, "Holy and blameless before him", and when it is a question of sonship, it is to Himself. It is a great thing for us to get hold of the fact that it is the blessed God and Father of our Lord Jesus Christ deliberating and considering in eternity what would be adequate to satisfy Himself, His own nature, in every way. In relation to God, counsel supposes a certain deliberation as to what is to be done; this thought is suggested on more than one occasion - He says to the children of Israel in the wilderness when they sinned, "Put off thine ornaments from thee, and I will know what I will do", Exodus 33:5. Think of God considering and deliberating, in the repose of eternity, what would satisfy His own mind and heart. It must be to have a people holy and blameless before Him in love, that is in the divine nature, morally suitable to Him. For the satisfaction of His heart relationship must be introduced; He must have sonship; He has marked us out beforehand for sonship. It is by Jesus Christ that God can bring everything to pass for His own pleasure. Jesus Christ is the One equal to bring it about; God has His own anointed Man who is able to bring it about. Think of a people in the conscious blessing of all this. God "has blessed us with every spiritual blessing in the heavenlies in Christ". This is not in purpose. It is in purpose that He chose us in Christ, but when He blesses us it suggests a company in the conscious joy of it.

Rem.   That would not be till the Spirit had come down?

C.A.C.   Quite so, and not till that had come to pass which was the fruit of the Spirit's coming down; the Spirit had His way with the saints in Ephesus. The fulness of all God was proposing could only be brought to a people who had a certain capacity to receive it. I do not think the epistle to Ephesus could have been sent to Corinth! There was a state of things at Ephesus which enabled the Lord through His servant to bring out this wonderful unfolding of the fulness of all that was in the mind and heart of God. It all depends on the presence of the Comforter, but at Ephesus things had taken such a course that there was a suitability for this to be unfolded to the saints there. Paul had laboured there and Timothy had been left there in order that the teaching and exhortations of Paul should take effect, and the first epistle to Timothy had taken effect so the house of God was seen in order at Ephesus. To an assembly in order the fullest blessing could be opened out, so it is a good thing for us to be orderly. If we read the epistles to the Corinthians, Galatians or even Colossians, there is something adverse or corrupting to be considered, but we do not get that in Ephesians; there is no adverse element present, so the fulness of all that is in the heart and mind of God can be brought out. The apostle turns to prayer on two occasions; it is only by prayer that we can get what he prays for. There are some things that can only be had by prayer; when things are put in the form of prayer, it suggests that is the way to arrive at them.

Ques.   Do heavenly blessings come through the burnt-offering aspect of the death of Christ? It is mentioned in chapter 5.

C.A.C.   The burnt-offering is connected with the walk of the saints there: "Walk in love, even as the Christ loved us, and delivered himself up for us, an offering and sacrifice to God for a sweet-smelling savour" (chapter 5: 2). It stands in relation to what the saints are on earth for the pleasure of God - that is how it is presented in Scripture. It is the new ground of acceptance for a people on earth, and it was the supreme expression of love on the part of Christ as found here for the pleasure of God. The burnt-offering is to be perpetuated in the saints; they are to walk in the same character, a character of sacrificial love in which one is prepared to suffer and surrender for the benefit of our fellow saints. I should think the heavenly blessings are connected with the sin-offering, because its blood went into the holy place; the blood of the burnt-offering never did. The sin-offering meets the glory of God in such an absolute way as to leave the blessed God a perfectly free hand so that He can have a company for heavenly blessing or for earthly blessing. He can do according to the good pleasure of His will because the sin-offering has so completely met His glory.

Ques. Do we get the sin-offering in Ephesians? Would it be in verse 7?

C.A.C. I think not. Of course redemption could not be apart from the sin-offering, but the apostle has developed the sin-offering in Romans, and it was not necessary to go over it again. He has set the blessedness of the sin-offering before us in Romans 3; Christ is there set forth, a mercy-seat on God's behalf through faith in His blood - that is the sin-offering. The character of the sin-offering is world-wide; it has a universal bearing because the blood is on the gold - on the mercy-seat, the throne of God. The glory of God in all its fulness is met by the blood of the sin-offering - that is the blood on the gold. The blood brought such eternal satisfaction to God of every claim necessitated by the condition which has come in through sin, so that God can carry out the good pleasure of His will, can justify sinners, can bring Israel into earthly blessing in the world to come, can bless the nations and in the assembly have a company in heavenly blessing. The blood of the sin-offering has met the glory of God, and based on it God can show Himself rich in mercy. In verse 7 it is the Person who is emphasised and though the blood is mentioned, it is in the Person that we have redemption. In verse 3 the blessings are in Christ, in verse 4 we are chosen in Him, and it is through Jesus Christ we are marked out for sonship, it is in the Beloved we are taken into favour, and we have redemption in Him. It is the greatness of Christ brought before us as the One by whom God can fill His own heart with delight and His universe with blessing; He has a Person great enough to do that. In this chapter we get faith in Christ in that character; not only as the Saviour who died to save poor sinners, but faith in Christ as the One great enough to fill the universe with divine pleasure; if He can do that He can fill my heart. The greater includes the less.

It is not the doctrine of the saints' acceptance in Christ here, but it is the Person of the Beloved that is before the heart, and the heart is consciously graced in Him. It is a great thing to get this Person before us.

God has chosen us in Christ to be holy and blameless before Him in love; that is what is suited to God as such. That corresponds with the God of our Lord Jesus Christ, but sonship corresponds with the Father of our Lord Jesus Christ. In John 20 the Lord says, "I ascend to my Father and your Father, and to my God and your God". There is a difference in the thought of His Father and God. If it is the thought of God everything must be morally suited to Him, there must be holiness and blamelessness, and the divine nature too. I think priesthood comes in in connection with "My God and your God", and sonship in connection with "My Father and your Father"; not that John develops sonship, but Paul does.

Ques.   Are the two prayers in Ephesians on that line? The first is to the God of glory and the second to the Father.

C.A.C.   That is it exactly. The two things go together: moral suitability is one thing, holiness, blamelessness and the divine nature; and on the other hand there is the relationship of sons, marked out beforehand for sonship. It is according to the good pleasure of His will to have us intelligent in what is a delight and joy to His heart - to have sons before Him. It is a profound pleasure to Him, it satisfies Him to have sons. It is to the praise of the glory of His grace. The transcendent character of His grace comes out; He graces us in the Beloved. There is a glorious Person before the face of God and the Father, He is designated the Beloved. The delight and love of God and the Father centre in that glorious Man, and the saints are privileged to know what it is to be graced in Him.

Ques.   Is it like John 17?

C.A.C.   "The glory which thou hast given me I have given them" is sonship. The glory is that in manhood He takes the place of Son; the place is given to Him so He can give it to others. He could not give what belonged to Him in eternity in the Godhead, but having this glory given to Him in manhood, the place of sonship before the Father, He can give it to others. We never get right thoughts of sonship save as seeing the place Christ has as Man. He has come into manhood and has taken such a place with His God and Father as no other man could. We have to learn the place of sonship in Him; we are marked out for it. The God and Father of our Lord Jesus Christ is the great Operator from eternity, and He has marked us out for it beforehand.

It is a wonderful thing that God should have a people set free to enter with wisdom and intelligence into all He has before Him; that is all connected with sonship. Redemption and forgiveness come in to make us perfectly free to enter into these great thoughts that God has before Him. "The mystery of his will" (verse 9) is that He is going to bring everything in heaven and earth to centre in Christ; He is going to head up everything in Christ. What a wonderful thought it is that we are set free by redemption and the knowledge of forgiveness so that we might enter with wisdom and intelligence into it all. Think of the greatness of Christ! There is a scene of confusion in heaven; Satan and his angels are there, and on earth there is lawlessness, so that both heaven and earth are in disorder. God is going to put it all in order by Christ, and is going to make everything centre in Christ for His satisfaction. What a glorious Person!

Ques.   Is it like Joseph's blessing?

C.A.C. Yes. "Unto the bounds of the everlasting hills", Genesis 49:26. You could not get beyond that, the blessings of heaven and earth. That is exactly what you do get here: a Man exalted at God's right hand is great enough to put the universe in order. If a poor sinner is in distress about sins you point him to Christ. One great enough to put heaven and earth in accord and make them answer to God's will is great enough to save me or any poor sinner.

Ques.   What are the riches of His grace? (verse 8).

C.A.C.   There is no expense too great for the wealth of His grace; that comes out in the blood. No price is too great for the blessed God to pay. The blood of this great Person has been shed; God gives any price to secure what He has set His heart on. That brings out the wealth of the grace of God; that is the riches of His grace. But the glory of His grace comes out in sonship. What a sight for the angels! They are sons of God, but they are not in sonship like the assembly. They are astonished and are waiting to see the assembly; they have heard a lot about it but they have not seen it. They will see it when it is presented a glorious assembly. There will be the presentation to Himself before the assembly is presented to the universe, before He displays the assembly to the universe and shows 'to wondering eyes that we with Him are one'. Before that He is going to present her to Himself, and she will be glorious, without a spot or wrinkle, not a mark of decrepitude or decay, not a single trace of unsuitability will be left. It is not only the result of redemption but the result of the washing of water by the word, and the nourishing and cherishing - she is going to come out as a glorious assembly.

Ques.   What is the "fulness of times"?

C.A.C.   It takes in all that we speak of as the world to come. Everything in heaven and earth will be caused to centre in Christ, to take character from Christ - that is the mystery of His will. It has been hidden a long time. It looks as if the devil did what he liked with heaven and earth, but it is not so at all! All is going to centre in Christ. There is a people who have pre-trusted in Christ; they have trusted beforehand, before things come into display in a day of glory. The remnant of Israel has pre-trusted before Israel as a whole has trusted in Him. The time is coming when Israel will trust, and the Gentiles will trust, but there is a special company who have pre-trusted; the saints on earth in the blessed secret of all Christ is going to be for the pleasure of God have trusted in this character. I think Paul links himself with the Jewish remnant who have trusted in Christ before the day of His glory while He is in reproach and rejection. It is that which gives a peculiar character to the present time; there is a people on earth in the time of His rejection who have trusted Him in regard to the place He is going to fill for the pleasure of God. We move through this world in the secret of Christ, God's anointed Man, who is going to bring to pass everything in heaven and earth for the pleasure of God; that would deliver us completely from the present course of things. This applies more particularly to the Jews who trust in Him beforehand. But then He turns to the Gentiles and says, You also have trusted in Him. So it applies to us, we have trusted beforehand, too, in the glory that has not come yet. This is the truth - that everything is to be headed up in Christ; He is great enough to put the whole universe into suitability to the pleasure of God; that is the One we have trusted in. If I have trusted Him as the One who is great enough to put the universe right, I have trusted Him as great enough to put me right, so it is "the glad tidings of your salvation". The One who can save the universe can save me; it is the glad tidings of salvation. What a Saviour! The Person who can put heaven and earth into suitability for the pleasure of God can put me and all who trust Him into suitability to God now. So we anticipate that day; Christ is great enough to make me right now; He is great enough to make me "holy and blameless", and great enough to introduce me and all saints into sonship in the presence of God. That is the Christ we trust; we cannot wonder that we are sealed. People with faith in Him are sealed with the Holy Spirit. The Spirit is given on that line as an earnest of the inheritance. It is in Christ we have the inheritance; everything in heaven and earth is going to be acquired by the Lord Jesus Christ; that is the inheritance. He has acquired possession in title, but not yet by freeing it by power; it has not yet been redeemed. He owns the title deeds; He has acquired possession as far as title goes, but He is going to free the inheritance from every encumbrance that rests upon it. It is in that Person that we have the inheritance, so what He has the saints have - we see that in Romans 8. In the interval before its being acquired, the joint heirs are being called, and they are going through suffering; they suffer with Christ and by and by they will be glorified. While they suffer they have for their comfort the joy of the inheritance by having the earnest of the Spirit. Before the inheritance is possessed in an outward way the joy of it is in the hearts of the saints by the Spirit; He is a part of it, the earnest of it; He brings the joy and blessing of the inheritance into the hearts of the suffering saints while they are waiting for redemption of the inheritance. That is the aspect of the Spirit here, not a seal to make me sure I am going to heaven.

———————

Reading 2 - *Probably at Teignmouth*
Ephesians 1:13-23

C.A.C.   We were seeing last week how the grace of our God has abounded to us in giving us wisdom and intelligence as to all that is before Himself. We must all realise that God could show no greater favour to His creatures than to bring them into the knowledge of Himself and give them intelligence as to all that is so precious to His own heart; it is the greatest conceivable favour. Christ was able to bring out by divine grace all that was in the blessed will of God. There is the good pleasure which God has purposed in Himself to bring everything in heaven and earth to find its centre and spring in Christ. It is a delightful thought for those who have been aware of the very different spring that has been operating. Things have been working in heaven and earth from a very different spring and source, but they are all going to be made to centre in Christ.

Rem.   God is the only Person who has a right to do as He likes, and this chapter shows what He does like to do.

C.A.C.   And what He does discloses what He is; it brings the very nature of God to light in a most blessed way after Satan has traduced and maligned Him for thousands of years, and after the creature is ready to accept every suggestion of the serpent and to believe that God is such a One who would turn him out of the garden for taking an apple! Well, God says, I am going to have a universe of bliss and I am going to give it to you. It is in Christ that the saints have obtained an inheritance, that wonderful Person who is great enough to fill the universe with pleasure for God. This gives a great enlargement to the thought of trusting in Christ. Trusting in Christ means that we have seen something of His trustworthiness.

He is so trustworthy that God can put everything under His hand and make everything under His hand to centre in Himself. He is the Man whom God trusts, and before the time comes when all this is brought into display there is a people who have trusted Him. While He is yet hidden out of sight there are those who trust Him according to the greatness of what He is able to effect. There is a Jewish and a Gentile company who have trusted Him before there is any outward manifestation of what He can do.

Rem.   Paul could say, "I know whom I

have believed, and am persuaded that he is able to keep for that day the deposit I have entrusted to him", 2 Timothy 1:12.

C.A.C. Yes, the apostle could trust Him absolutely; he did not need to trouble about his own vindication or his reputation; he committed it altogether to the Lord. Saints had turned away from Paul; he was in great reproach among the brethren, a lonely aged prisoner, but he knew the One he had believed, and he had committed everything to Him.

Rem. And he sang praises all the way through.

C.A.C. When we get the sense of having an inheritance we get the joy of it and are able to praise God for it; we become delightful to God in a practical sense as we take up God's thoughts and purposes in Christ. God will bring Israel into the earthly inheritance. He never abandoned His title; it is still Immanuel's land. They will be brought into the earthly inheritance, and when they take it up in correspondence with the thoughts of God they will be delightful to God. How wonderful that they should take it up as Immanuel's land, the land belonging to the One who is God with us! There is no doubt the faith of the Old Testament saints took account of Christ and so they could be spoken of as the dead in Christ.

Ques.   What is the feature of the Gentiles trusting in Christ?

C.A.C.   It is connected with the character of the mystery as developed in this epistle. The mystery is that the Gentiles should be fellow-heirs and partakers of the heavenly calling. There is not only a Jewish company who trusted before the time when the nations will be in display, but also a Gentile company who have pre-trusted before there is any manifestation of what He can do in the universe. They heard the word of truth, the "glad tidings of your salvation", and it becomes the means of complete deliverance from the present course of things. It is much greater than getting our own burden lifted; it is complete deliverance from all the evils rampant in the Gentile world; that is what the gospel of our salvation means, and it is all brought about by trusting in the Christ, in the greatness of the Christ, and what He can do for the pleasure of God. It delivers the soul from Jewish and Gentile evil. It is not simply that evil is judged; John the baptist got as far as that. It is very interesting to see the history of these Ephesians. When Paul first got to Ephesus, he found twelve men, disciples; they had not the Spirit; they had been baptised with John's baptism which only went as far as repentance and the judgment of evil that characterises everything here. Evil will not do for God. John went as far as that, but he spoke of Another coming in who could set up all for the pleasure of God. The Ephesians had to move on to faith in Christ as the One coming after John who could bring in everything for the pleasure of God. When they trusted in Him they got the Spirit.

Ques. Why is He called the Spirit of promise?

C.A.C. I think the Spirit is the great promise; I do not know anything greater promised in the Old Testament; it is the supreme promise there - "I will put my Spirit upon him", Isaiah 42:1. And in every gospel John the baptist announced Christ as the One who would baptise with the Spirit. When the Lord's ministry closes He speaks much of the Comforter. The first promise of God to men now is the Spirit. Those who have faith in Christ are sealed; trusting in Him and believing in Him they are sealed with the Holy Spirit of promise. Everything on our side is dependent on the presence of the Spirit. The greatness of Christ is that He can baptise, immerse in the Holy Spirit. I do not know if we realise the greatness of the baptism in the Holy Spirit. Christ is great enough to take His people, those who believe on Him and immerse them in the Holy Spirit. I can think of nothing of greater importance than to see the greatness of Christ in relation to the Holy Spirit. He does not leave those who believe on Him in the region of flesh, or the world, or human thoughts and feelings, but He takes them and immerses them in the Holy Spirit. It is good to be put into the greatness of divine things. Here it comes in as marking the saints off for the inheritance - that is the point. The saints are marked off for the inheritance by the sealing, and the same wonderful Person becomes the earnest of the inheritance.

Ques.   Is it what Christ inherits as Man?

C.A.C.   I think so. The purpose which God purposed in Himself is that He is going to make everything in heaven and earth centre in Christ and that is given to the saints as their inheritance; it constitutes the wealth of God. The universe filled out of Christ, made to centre in Christ, constitutes the wealth of God, and He is going to enjoy all He possesses by putting His saints in possession of it. To produce a universe of bliss which finds its centre in Christ and is filled out of the fulness of Christ does not satisfy the heart of the blessed God. To have an estate does not satisfy anyone; the greater the estate a man has, the more desire he has for an heir. We all know in our experience that if we take great delight in anything, our joy is greatly intensified if we have someone to share it. Now that is exactly the joy of the blessed God; He is going to have a company of sons to participate in the joy He has brought about and is going to bring about in Christ. The supreme joy of God will be in the joy of sons who can enter intelligently and in their affections with common interest into the inheritance; that will satisfy the heart of God. The prayer at the end of the chapter comes in in connection with this. The apostle prays for something in addition to the sealing and earnest of the Spirit. He does not pray that they may have the sealing or the earnest, they have that, but he prays for something additional, the spirit of wisdom and revelation. He gets down on his knees and prays that they might have the "spirit of wisdom and revelation in the full knowledge of him", that there should be a power in the saints to know the nature of God and what God can delight in. We can only know it in a kindred nature.

Ques.   Is that Colossians?

C.A.C.   That is the start, there was a measure of formation in the divine nature in them, and when it is there there is something to work on.

Ques. Should it be constant faith or believing?

C.A.C. Yes. In John's gospel the word believing is always used as characteristic of the believer. It is not that we have heard the gospel some twenty years ago and believed it - that does not constitute one a believer in John's way, but the person is a believing one; that marks him. The Lord said before He went away, "Ye believe on God, believe also on me"; He is to be the abiding Object of faith. The gospel of John was written that "ye may believe ... and that believing ye might have life in his name", John 20:31.

Ques. If as believers we had faith in the Lord Jesus would not every difficulty be solved?

C.A.C. I think so. It would settle everything because there is such a resource in Him, an unfailing Person. Then love to all the saints would show the divine nature in activity; one who loves all saints is no longer alienated from the life of God.

Ques. The apostle did not cease giving thanks for them. Was that because he had found a company to whom he could give the choicest thoughts of God?

C.A.C. Yes, and yet there was something

very great for them to be still endowed with. Though they were in such an excellent state yet he prays that God would give them the spirit of wisdom and revelation in the knowledge of Him. The spirit of revelation is a remarkable expression, it is not only a spirit of wisdom but of revelation. It is something in the saints that corresponds with all the blessedness of the revelation that has come; it is not only known as ministered to us, but actually known because there is something there in keeping with it in the believer. It is beautiful but immense. It is a question of what we know; we get the "full knowledge of him" in verse 17, and "so that ye should know what is the hope of his calling" in verse 18. There are things that cannot be known by reading them in Scripture. We might think by reading this chapter we could get to know these things, but we cannot know them that way. People often think that if they study Scripture sufficiently they would get to know divine things, but they are known by the spirit of wisdom and revelation. It is the God of our Lord Jesus Christ, the Father of glory, the wonderful Originator of the whole system of glory, who can give to us a spirit of wisdom and revelation so that we may know Him in relation to the vast system of glory which He has purposed in Christ. The spirit of wisdom and revelation can be had by asking, no one need be without it.

Ques.   Is it the quickening?

C.A.C.   We get that in the next chapter. In this prayer it is a question of knowing rather than living; quickening is living. Knowing comes first. A great deal of Christian blessing lies in knowledge; life eternal lies in knowledge, and "we know that the Son of God has come", 1 John 5: 20. This knowledge is a wonderful thing - to know the hope of His calling, His inheritance in the saints and the surpassing greatness of His power towards us which was manifested in the resurrection of Christ - to know these things is immense, the natural mind could not take in any of them. The eyes of your heart being enlightened indicates that the affections are illuminated; the heart is illuminated by the light of it all. The Father of glory is the Originator of the whole system of glory and He is the One who delights to give His saints the spirit of wisdom and revelation so that they might know Him in that character.

Ques.   What about the eyes of our hearts?

C.A.C.   I think it suggests the affections have perceptive power as divinely illuminated. It is not merely getting hold of things mentally, but there is divine illumination in the heart. God is love and none of the wisdom of God can be understood except by love, so the eyes of the heart need to be enlightened.

Ques.   What is the hope of His calling?

C.A.C.   It is the whole vast scene of glory which is in the good pleasure of God to bring about, what He purposed to bring about. What He purposed in Himself is a matter of hope - all is in hope as yet.

———————

Reading 3 - *Probably at Teignmouth*

Ephesians 1:15-23; Ephesians 2:1-10

C.A.C.   It is well for us to ponder deeply the things which God would have us to know. One might well ask oneself, 'How much do I know the riches of the glory of His inheritance in the saints?' God would have us to know by the spirit of wisdom and revelation what a portion He has in His saints. It is wonderful to think of God having any inheritance at all, that there should be anything spoken of as an inheritance for God. An inheritance suggests a thought of something that has to be waited for for a certain definite time and then it can be enjoyed. Now that is the position in relation to God; He has waited a long time for His inheritance. The thought was suggested in the Old Testament of His people being His inheritance; there are a good many scriptures that give us this idea, "Israel mine inheritance", Isaiah 19:25. But God never got His inheritance till Christ had died and risen and gone to His right hand. When the saints are brought in spiritual power to the blessedness of what is in Christ, then God gets His inheritance in them. It is good to see that God could not enjoy what He has proposed and brought about in Christ; He must have the saints in it before He can enjoy it. That is the thought in this Scripture. Of course, He established it all in Christ in view of the saints coming in and enjoying it; the way God gets the joy and the possession of the inheritance is by bringing His saints into it.

Ques. What is the thought of the inheritance?

C.A.C. Everything which God has purposed in Christ.

Ques. Is it a present thing?

C.A.C. Yes, that is what it means when it speaks of the riches of the glory of the inheritance in the saints. God enjoys the inheritance in the saints of the assembly. It is just as we can take up and enter into the great and blessed thoughts that God has been establishing in Christ, and as we enter in and become possessed of them, that we become pleasurable to God as His inheritance. He gets the joy of all He has established in Christ by bringing the saints into it.

The fact of the apostle praying in this way shows how great the inheritance is; it requires the spirit of wisdom and revelation and for the eyes of our hearts to be enlightened so that we may know it. It requires the most wonderful action on God's part so that the saints should know it. We cannot get it by reading Scripture. We might read Ephesians 1 every morning, noon and night for a lifetime and never know it; it is only known by having from God the spirit of wisdom and revelation and the eyes of our hearts enlightened; then we know these things and never till then. Then we know what the hope of His calling is, that vast scene of glory that is going to be headed up in Christ. It is possible for the saints to know it spiritually and then to know what a portion God has in His saints by bringing them into all the fulness that He has established in Christ.

If we can speak to God with intelligent knowledge of what He has established in Christ in such a way that He sees we have possession of it, He has great pleasure in us, we become His inheritance. What a thought that the saints are indispensable to the joy of the Godhead! We must pray if we want to know it; there is no other way. Having readings shows us what there is to get, and if they work rightly they send us to our knees, and then we pray and get the things spiritually. It is not simple information, we all have that because we are familiar with the Scriptures, but how much have we got in our souls in spiritual power? That is quite another thing. I only know what I know by the spirit of wisdom and revelation and the eyes of my heart being enlightened. There is the greatest encouragement in all this, because God does not put these things before us to make us think it is all over our heads. We hear saints talking about its being over their heads; what a mercy if there is something over our heads! It is a poor look-out if things are not over our heads; they are over our heads to draw us up to them. God shows us something far above our thoughts and conceptions in order that we may see that it is ours to go in for. If it is above my head the sooner I get up to it the better. We get it through exercise and the operation of divine knowledge; it is not what a schoolmaster could teach. The epistle supposes the condition of soul is there - faith in the Lord Jesus and love to all the saints in order that there should be a proper foundation on which to work. They had been sealed with the Holy Spirit of promise and had the earnest of the inheritance. They had got a portion in having the Spirit, and what they wanted was a further accession. The spirit of wisdom and revelation is something additional to the gift of the Spirit. We enter on Christianity proper by having the Spirit; no one could even be a babe in Christ if he had not the Spirit, but that is the threshold of Christianity; there is the further gift, the spirit of wisdom and revelation. We need our hearts to be stirred up to see how much there is to go in for - we stop with such a small measure of things.

In chapter 1 it is the pleasure of God; it is His purpose and glory, and in chapter 2 it is the power by which He gives effect to His purpose and glory; it is what God is doing for His pleasure. If we do not want to give pleasure to God we may as well shut up this book, but if we are on the line of divine pleasure we shall be very interested in it. It is the full light of the heavenly position and, of course, above our heads but it need not be above our hearts. God would put us into harmony with the way He is working; He is working along a certain line. The second chapter looks at what God is working for in its completeness. He has raised us up together, and we are sitting together in heavenly places; evidently that is the complete thing. We have the full light of divine purpose and divine power which can put the saints into it; it is all looked at as complete, though not complete in me. It should surely fill our hearts with the sense of the greatness of Christ. We see at the end of the chapter the greatness of Christ's present position; it is what God has done with Him. It is a little different from Colossians; there it is the greatness of Christ personally, here it is the greatness of Christ in the position that

God has given Him; it is what God has done with Christ. "Set him ... far above all ...". (A.V.) is the place that God has given Him, so there is a need with us for knowing the surpassing character of God's power, the great power that wrought in Christ when He raised Him from the dead; that is the power that operates towards us at this moment.

Ques. Would Christ have inherited apart from the fall?

C.A.C. I do not see how He could have. The coming of Christ and His going down to death was part of the divine counsel, though the occasion of it was the fall of man, and so the wisdom of God is seen in all He permitted to transpire in connection with Satan's power and with death. It provided that on which God could work out His own counsel and purposes; that is where the greatness of God's power comes in. None of us has a connection of it apart from the spirit of wisdom and revelation. No one can get an idea of resurrection apart from that, for resurrection is outside the scope of the human mind. Everyone in Christendom professes to know what it means but they do not; man's mind is not capable of taking it in. Man can understand the immortality of the soul, but he has no idea of resurrection; it is the mighty power of God. The power of

His resurrection is wonderful. There was a Man in death - Christ - and the surpassing greatness of God's power has been seen in the fact that He wrought in that dead Man; the might of His strength wrought there and He raised Him from the dead. It was the greatest act of divine power that ever took place or ever will take place. There was never such an act of divine power as the raising of that dead Man. We get the ground cleared by His death - sin is judged, death annulled, Satan's power broken, principalities and powers spoilt, God glorified, man redeemed, everything is settled in the death of Christ, and now we get the power of God beginning an entirely new sense so there is a Man raised out of death. That is the power that operates towards the saints; the power that began operating in the raising of Christ has gone on and never ceases to act towards the saints. The power is always working towards those who believe to bring them into the sphere where divine power is working.

The apostle's prayer ends in the middle of verse 20, "In raising him from among the dead" - that is the end of the prayer. Then the apostle goes on with his teaching, "And he set him down at his right hand"; he goes on to tell them what God did with Him after He raised Him.

Ques. Is it anything like "Thy people shall be willing in the day of thy power", Psalm 110:3?

C.A.C. That shows the power of God put forth to make His people free-will offerings. God's power is put forth that His people may move freely in relation to Himself. That is what we get here, the mighty power operating towards the saints that they may move in light towards God and become free-will offerings, a glad surrender to God for His pleasure.

Quickening means we are made to live together with Christ - what a wonderful thing to think of! One longs to know what it means. One sees the wonderful place God has given to Christ, and that same power that raised Him and set Him in such a lofty position is operating in the saints to bring them up to the same level - the saints are to go up to the same level.

Ques. Is it in a subjective way with us?

C.A.C. Yes, exactly.

Rem. It used to be looked at as purpose that we are quickened and set there.

C.A.C. It is more than purpose, it is purpose carried into effect. It is purpose in chapter 1, "Chosen us in him before the world's foundation, that we should be holy and blameless before him in love; having marked us out beforehand for adoption through Jesus Christ to himself" (verses 4, 5). All that is purpose, and it is absolute before the foundation of the world. But the saints being quickened in power is not purpose. If I am quickened, there has been an operation of divine power in me. We ought to take in the thought of it; God brings it before us. God shows us the wonderful place He has given to Christ, He has placed Him at this present moment "above every principality, and authority, and power, and dominion, and every name named, not only in this age, but also in that to come". That is Christ's present place, that is where He is at this moment. The only Christ there is is the One there. There is no Christ in humiliation or resurrection now; the only Christ there is is ascended and seated at the right hand of God. We could not sit with Him in the heavenlies if we were not quickened. The very fact that it is presented as what God is effecting ought to move our hearts. I cannot quicken myself, but it is something to let the light into our hearts. God is operating in the way of quickening power. It is difficult to get hold of because it is presented here in its completeness as actually accomplished in Jew and Gentile.

Ques.   What does quickening imply?

C.A.C. It means being made to live. If I have been made to live together with Christ it is a blessed reality brought about in my affections. The only way we are quickened now is in our affections, our bodies are not quickened yet; when the Lord comes they will be made to live in spiritual life on account of the Spirit dwelling in them (Romans 8), but before that the affections of the saints are quickened so that they can live together with the Christ, who is a glorified Man at the right hand of God. The saints in affection are made to live in that scene and association. Practically we touch it a bit now and then but there is no reason why it should be only a momentary thing.

Ques. Do you make the quickening of the body entirely future?

C.A.C. There may be a moral sense in which the body is quickened so that it can be presented a living sacrifice. In that sense you can speak of it as quickened for the service of God so that instead of the body being a vessel for the deeds of the flesh it becomes a vessel for the will of God. But Romans 8 contemplates the full result in the mortal bodies of saints; they will be quickened when the Lord comes. Quickening gives one the idea that Christian blessedness is not in relation to things on earth but in relation to a glorious Person who is above all principalities and powers and every name that is named, and He is Head over all things to the assembly. He has that character in the eyes of the assembly, it cherishes Him as Head over all things.

Ques. What is the thought of sitting together?

C.A.C. It indicates the perfect repose in which Jew and Gentile can occupy the heavenly position. It is a definite position, not what we have to move from; any other position we occupy on earth, even risen with Christ, we have to move from. We do not sit as risen with Christ; we have to move from that position. It does not represent the full thought of God and hence would not be an abiding place for us. It is not ascension; it is not like being in the full light of the heavenly position. When we get to that there is no movement so we sit, it is an abiding place for the saints; there is no further stage in their journey; they have reached the terminus. In Colossians you have not reached the terminus. It is blessed to be risen with Christ; there is nothing more blessed on earth, but in Colossians you are looking up to heaven. The assembly has a position as risen with Christ, but that is not the full thought of God, so you do not sit as risen with Christ, you stand as gazing up to heaven, "Have your mind on the things that are above, not on the things that are on the earth" (Colossians 3:2), but when you get to heaven you sit. The Lord is very particular in John to call their attention to Himself as the ascending One. He does not say, 'I am the risen One, go to my brethren', but He says, "I ascend". That is His character. It is not that He is going to ascend but He has ascended. That is the full light of the position, as the ascending One He comes into the midst.

The body comes in in verse 23 as the body of that glorious Person who is in such an elevated position; it is the fulness of Him who fills all in all - it is inconceivable! If God did not bring it before us we should think it incredible that there could be such a thing. We see the immensity of this Person and the elevated position He is in, and then we find there is a company which is His fulness, a company of persons adequate to the setting Him forth as His body - it is stupendous! One cannot wonder that so many Christians do not enter into the thought of the assembly. We do not, though it is constantly brought before us. We get a dim thought of it occasionally, but rather as light. Think of the assembly as the fulness of Him who filleth all in all! Jew and Gentile both one body in Christ, a company of persons adequate to set Him forth as His body! It makes one feel that nothing but the quickening power of God could bring that about; it could not be by human power, so the assembly is a divine formation. There is no natural or human thought in the assembly as viewed in Ephesians; it is purely of divine formation.

Ques. What is the thought of filling all in all?

C.A.C. That the whole universe is going to be filled out of the blessedness of Christ, and it is not only going to be characterised by what He is actually but by what He is internally, so He fills all in all. It is not only the character of Christ that will be expressed externally in every part of the moral universe, but it will be there internally; the spirit of everything will be derived from Christ. Fancy all the sensibilities in the universe made like Christ, every intelligent being in God's moral universe thinking like Christ, feeling like Christ, having emotions and sensibilities like Christ! What pleasure to God! That is the measure of the stature of the fulness of the Christ, and God will never be satisfied until He has brought it about. It is going on feebly on our side now, but tremendous divine power is working to bring it about, and the assembly will come out in glory as the fulness of Christ. Think what it will be for God; one can hardly imagine it! God has had a universe in which sin has come in; Satan's power and death have come in too. He has another universe where everything will carry an impression of Christ. Ephesians 1 gives a sense of what there is for God, and chapter 2 goes on to show how His power works so that He can raise the saints as quickened to the same elevation as Christ. Then they come at the end of chapter 2 to be "a habitation of God in the Spirit". If we do not get away from the thought of blessing for man, we shall fail to enter into these things; we are very slow to take in God's side, what is for Him. Nothing but God's quickening power will take us away from ourselves.

What a contrast this is to what we were, "dead in your offences and sins - in which ye once walked according to the age of this world, according to the ruler of the authority of the air, the spirit who now works in the sons of disobedience". There is a moral atmosphere in the world and it is marked by disobedience and fulfilling the desires of the flesh and mind. That is the atmosphere of the world, we lived there once and we know it is true because living there we were children of wrath. We were of such a character that nothing but wrath could attach to us, creatures that did their own will and would not give God a place at all, "children, by nature, of wrath … (we too being dead in offences)". What was there on God's part? He was "rich in mercy" and He has "great love wherewith he loved us". The old woman was right when she said that she knew God loved her before she was born for there had been nothing to love since!

"Ye are saved by grace" - what a wonderful salvation! "Quickened … with the Christ" is the complete thought of salvation. There is always a tendency with us to revert to our old history but in the light of Ephesians it would not be possible.

———————

Reading 4 - *26 April 1917*
Probably at Teignmouth
Ephesians 1:15-23; Ephesians 2:11-17

Ques.   Do we get as wide a view here of the death of Christ as in Colossians 1?

C.A.C. The wide view is brought out in verse 10; all things are to be headed up in the Christ, things in heaven and on earth. Then, when the assembly is in view in verse 22, He is "head over all things to the assembly". That takes in the wide scope of His glory, does it not? It is very encouraging to see the greatness of God's power; we could hardly entertain anything in this epistle if we had not regard to that. It is very striking that the greatness of God's power should come out in relation to death. That is the first aspect of the death of Christ that is presented here, it is death that has been the occasion of bringing out the surpassing greatness of God's power. Instead of death being a scene of the enemy's power and of the weakness of the creature, it has become the most wonderful witness ever known in the universe of the surpassing greatness of God's power. How He has reversed everything!

Ques.   In verse 17, does the "knowledge of him" refer to God or Christ?

C.A.C.   It is the knowledge of God, the spirit of wisdom and revelation in the full knowledge of the God of our Lord Jesus Christ.

Rem.   So we must start with the knowledge of the God of our Lord Jesus Christ.

C.A.C.   That is what is being effected now by the mighty power of God. It is not the power of creation; our greatest natural conception of power is creation. We think of God as Almighty and of creation as the greatest expression of His power, but it is not so. We have to learn to think of God's power in another way; it has come out in raising a Man from the dead. We ought to ponder these things, they give one an idea of power working in a sphere entirely outside of what is of man, and one gets the feeling one can expect anything after that! There is no thought that can be suggested, or that can come in on God's part that is too great to be carried out. God puts resurrection before us as the greatest act of His power. He would have it known. Death is utter weakness; when Christ lay in the absolute weakness of death, then God's power came in.

Ques. Is resurrection greater than redemption?

C.A.C.   Redemption is not complete without resurrection. Redemption is God acting in power for the recovery of what has been lost, and you not only need the blood for it but you need the power of resurrection. In Exodus 15 it was the people on the resurrection side of the Red Sea who could say, "The people that thou hast redeemed" (verse 13). Death is not enough; you must be in victory and you must have something to put away death. Death comes in to put away sin, but the mighty power of God comes in to put away death by resurrection. You cannot think of one without the other. That mighty power had us in view; God was not thinking of Himself alone, He was bringing His power to light towards us who believe. The assembly is in a special way the witness to all this. The full fruit of the death of Christ and of the power of God will not come out in any company as it does in the assembly. The assembly has a peculiar place as a vessel of divine fulness, "That ye may be filled even to all the fulness of God" (chapter 3: 19). We were speaking last week about the fulness reconciling all things to itself, but Ephesians suggests another thought, that there is going to be a vessel for the display of the fulness. It will not come out in Israel or in any other company. Some part may come out in Israel but what a marvellous creation the assembly is! It is created in the mighty power that raised Christ from the dead. People say that too much is made of the assembly, but if they saw what God has made and will make of the assembly, they would see it is impossible to make too much of her. People look at the assembly on man's side as if it were something man had organised, but it is all of God and derives everything from Christ. If it is a vessel for the display of God's glory and for the display of Christ, then we can go a long way without making too much of her. If we only look at her from man's side, it is merely a human way of thinking.

Rem.   I suppose it arises from thinking of the assembly as ourselves.

C.A.C.   We should be like Laodicea if we thought of the assembly as ourselves. No, we must have our view filled with the God of our Lord Jesus Christ and in the knowledge of Him we arrive at the assembly.

Rem.   He is the Father of glory.

C.A.C.   That is, it all originates with Him; everything in the expanse of glory originates with the God of our Lord Jesus Christ. In Laodicea we get the Lord presented as "the beginning of the creation of God". That should have preserved them. If they had had a sense of that there would have been no vainglory. Laodicea was boasting of what the church was, with her true riches, God, Christ and the Spirit, all left out.

It is striking that the next presentation of the death of Christ is what brings men together; this is in order for God to have pleasure in men so as to dwell in them; they must be brought into proper unity and the death of Christ is the divine way of bringing that about. We are not enough concerned about getting close to one another. The dwelling of God here is dependent on our being builded together, and that certainly means being in close contact.

Rem. Distance exists today amongst Christians. We think of it with the Jew and Gentile as a historical fact, but the spirit of it exists today.

C.A.C. Yes, we have to take it up in a moral way. We read a scripture like this too dispensationally, as if it were merely that the Jew and Gentile had been brought together in the ways of God, but what about you and me? You may be a Jew and I a Gentile figuratively. If as saints we do not apprehend the death of Christ in the way it is presented here, it shows we are some distance apart.

Rem.   When we come together we are tested in relation to one another. The measure in which we hold the truth will expose itself.

C.A.C.   If we are to walk here in consistency with this presentation of truth we must learn the death of Christ in this character. If I really learnt the import of the death of Christ, there would be nothing to cause a shade of difference between me and another Christian who has learned it, so we could get into the closest possible contact. We are made one, an organic unity. One feels ashamed to read Ephesians from our side; it is blessed from God's side. What a dwelling for God, people with not a shade between them! At Pentecost there were three thousand people and only one mind. God's thought is a dwelling place for Himself composed of those builded together, the things that would keep us apart all done away in the death of Christ. There were two men before God, Jew and Gentile, and Christ went into death to close the history of both of them, and to end what had been enmity (God's law and ordinances) between them. God says, 'What has been enmity I am going to set aside, I want your hearts in unity, because I am going to dwell among you'. It almost appeared of old as if God was the God of the Jews, and the devil was the god of the Gentiles, but now God has done away with all that. Oh, the power of the death of Christ if it takes away the man after the flesh! It is the man after the flesh that is to be removed whether I am a good man or a bad man, whether I am a nice man or a nasty man! We have all our natural peculiarities, things that are like angular points that keep us from contact with one another, but that is the man after the flesh. If this is all gone and our souls have learnt the death of Christ, nothing can keep us apart.

Rem.   Reserve between saints is a witness that we are not in liberty.

C.A.C.   Satan is working to bring in elements of discord. I think spots and wrinkles (chapter 5: 27) are elements of discord; they spoil the beauty of the assembly. The beauty of the assembly is her unity, and the devil says, 'I will bring in as many blemishes and spots as possible to spoil the beauty of the bride'. She is one pearl, a perfect unity. Satan works with each of us to spoil beauty. If he can bring in something fleshly with any of us, there is an element that disturbs unity and the beauty is spoilt.

It is interesting to see the privilege side and the testimony side. The privilege side is that we have access to the Father, and the testimony side is that we are a habitation of God.

We should ponder the death of Christ more. We try to put things right without using divine means. It is only as we ponder the death of Christ and drink in its import that we shall find every element of discord rebuked. We all admit saints should be in unity; we accept it as a principle, but we do not sufficiently ponder the death of Christ as the power to bring it about.

Ques.   Do we look at unity as the divine mind for us, or do we only mourn our discord in the assembly for the shame of what we are in the eyes of man?

C.A.C.   If we do not see the divine thought of the assembly, we shall never see the complete ruin of the assembly in the hands of man. It is such a ruin under the eye of God, not only in testimony, but we can get back to the original thought. The saints at Ephesus were prepared by the work of God in them to appreciate what is presented; they were spiritually capable of entertaining it. It is an immense thing to be in a state that qualifies one to appreciate the full height of God's thoughts, an immense privilege. We should pray that it might be true of us. It is a very real thing to be taken into God's confidence as to that which is so exceedingly precious to Him. One cannot imagine the profound and intense interest of the blessed God in all this, and there could not be any favour so great as to be taken into His confidence.

———————

Address at Ventnor

7 February 1899

Ephesians 2:4-22

I suppose every Christian must be conscious that there is peculiar fulness and blessedness in the truth as presented in this epistle. We have things unfolded here as they are in the mind of God; the ministry is not limited by any consideration of feebleness or failure in saints.

The first chapter is chiefly connected with "the God of our Lord Jesus Christ, the Father of glory" (verse 17). I understand the use of this name conveys the thought that God is the Author and Originator of a circle of things characterised by glory. It is a scene of glory that is brought before us where everything is headed up in Christ. We are brought in according to God's eternal choice and the good pleasure of His will to obtain an inheritance in Christ "to the praise of his glory" (verses 12, 14). God has marked us out for sonship in a universe of bliss. And as the bride of Christ the assembly will inherit everything in Him and with Him.

Then we get the power by which all this is effected. There is no doubt that man has gone from the lowest place in God's universe to the highest place by "the working of the might" of God's strength. The Lord Jesus came into death for us to maintain the glory of God in respect of all that we had done and all that we were, and God's mighty power came in and raised Him from the dead and set Him in the highest place in the universe. It is that power that is "towards us who believe". Nothing less than that power could take us up from death and put us in the heavenlies in Christ.

In chapter 1 we see that God has marked us out for sonship "to the praise of the glory of his grace", and we have obtained an inheritance in Christ that "we should be to the praise of his glory"; but in chapter 2 we see what God is doing for the satisfaction of His love.

"God, being rich in mercy" comes in because of our state and condition; nothing but the wealth of mercy could have met us, but on God's side it is "because of his great love wherewith he loved us". God has taken us up, not only in the depth of mercy, but to satisfy His own love.

There are three wonderful and blessed things stated in connection with this: He "has quickened us with the Christ" (verse 5), He "has raised us up together, and has made us sit down together in the heavenlies in Christ Jesus" (verse 6). The object in view in all this is that we may be brought consciously into the presence of the holy love of God.

In Old Testament times men were not in the presence of the love of God. I have no doubt the Old Testament saints knew something of God as being rich in mercy, but it was impossible they could know Him in the satisfaction of His love. The reason is simple: the Object which alone could furnish satisfaction to the love of God was not yet revealed. But when the Son of God came here "the heaven was opened ... and a voice came out of heaven, Thou art my beloved Son, in thee I have found my delight", Luke 3:21, 22. The Father's love found its perfect repose in that blessed One, and He found His repose in the love of which he was the Object - He was "in the bosom of the Father" (John 1:18).

But the beloved Son was alone in the presence of the Father's love. If we were to be brought into it He must die; there was necessity for our sinful flesh to be removed. The death and judgment due to us have come upon Him. Sinful flesh could not be brought into the presence of God's love, but it has been condemned in the death of

Christ; and another thing, that condition of being, human life in flesh and blood, with which in us sin and death have come into contact, has been brought to an end before God in the death of Christ. The end of all flesh has come before God.

And when Christ rose from the dead it was in an entirely new state - quickened in the Spirit; it is a state with which sin and death never had, and never can have, any contact whatever, "In that he lives, he lives to God", Romans 6:10. He is for ever absolutely apart from every question of sin and death, having taken up all those questions once at the cross for the glory of God. He now lives in resurrection in the presence of God's holy love.

The great thing for us is to see that God would bring us to live together with Him in the presence of that wondrous love. To be quickened together with Christ is to be made to live in spirit outside everything that has been touched by sin or that has come under death in the presence of God's holy love. How we are brought into this may be seen in John 20:15-18; John 20:22. In the first place there was a ministry which gave the disciples the light of an entirely new association with Christ as the risen One. This was in the message sent by Mary. Then when He breathed into them I think it was in figure, bringing them into the consciousness of their associations with Him. We get the light of things through ministry but we only get the consciousness of them as we are energised by the Spirit in the affections of our inward man.

Mary is, in a certain way, a figure of gift; she was the great apostle of Christianity to the apostles. I think the Lord sent this message by a woman to show that in connection with His things affection is the chief qualification. It was love that qualified Mary to receive this message and to carry it. She was not required to add anything to it. The most important qualification of a gift is the jealousy of love that the message should not be marred in any way. When the light came to them they were affected by it. If we are rightly affected by divine light we shall soon get the consciousness of what is presented to us as light. The light conveyed in Mary's message put the disciples outside what was of man, and gathered them together with the doors shut upon the religious man according to the flesh, that is, the Jews. Then the Lord came and stood in the midst, and after speaking peace to them, and showing them His hands and His side, He breathed into them. He imparted to them, in figure, the consciousness of being in association with

Him in life. He would have them to know that they lived with Him in the presence of the Father's love.

Then God has "raised us up together"; the idea is that we are lifted entirely off the earth. Jew and Gentile lifted up in spirit into an entirely new atmosphere, where all the old distinctions are left behind. I have read that all the storms are on the surface of the earth, and that it is an eternal calm when an elevation of six or seven miles is reached. God would lift us up in spirit above the region of storms - above the things that are here. We have responsibilities down here and often we get worried and anxious about them, but we ought to know what it is to live above. 'Business below, residence above' was on a Christian's door-plate, and it is good to have it so in a spiritual way. Mr. Stoney used to compare the Christian to a man going up in a balloon and losing his natural senses but getting a new and spiritual sense suited to the new scene to which he was introduced. God would carry us up in spirit to the region where Christ is. There are no politics or nationalities or worries there. We have all heard the story of the cobbler of whom his wife said that he lived in heaven and only came down here to mend shoes! "And has made us sit down together in the heavenlies in Christ

Jesus". God would have us in perfect repose in a scene of absolute rest, and there in the presence of His love and for the satisfaction of that love. Of course, it is in spirit only that this can be realised now, but God gives effect to it with a view to bringing into display the surpassing riches of His grace in the ages to come.

The result of apprehending all this is that we come out in a new character down here; we enter upon our calling. There is one new man and one body; we have access to the Father and we are builded together for a habitation of God in the Spirit. What marks the new man is that he takes his character from God (chapter 4: 24). It takes all the saints on earth to make up and express the new man. Then the great privilege of Christianity is access to the Father. God is fully revealed in love and we approach Him through Christ and by one Spirit. We go to Him in all the sweet savour of Christ and have the consciousness of this by the Spirit.

Then lastly, we are builded together for a habitation of God. This is our testimony. God dwells here in grace and blessing in His house; He is known in His saints. Many things might suit us, but do they express what is of God? The fact that we are God's habitation has a most practical bearing in this way. The whole company of saints on earth form the habitation of God and each individual believer is responsible to be true to his character as forming part of that holy habitation.

———

Word at Teignmouth

29 May 1904

Ephesians 3:14-17

Christ dwells in the Father's heart and fills it. When here in flesh, handled and contemplated by the apostles, He was "with the Father" - "the only-begotten Son, who is in the bosom of the Father" (John 1:18). He ever dwelt in the Father's affections. Paul would have Christ to dwell in our hearts also, and to this end he bows his knees to the Father, desiring that we may be strengthened with power by the Father's Spirit in the inner man. This is the only scripture where the Holy Spirit is spoken of as the Spirit of the Father (In Matthew 10:20 it is "thc Spirit of your Father" - a different thought). If we are strengthened by the Father's Spirit, the One who dwells in the Father's heart will dwell in our hearts. Our faith will be strengthened to hold that blessed One in abiding occupation of our affections.

If the apostle bowed his knees to the Father about this, is it not fitting that we should do likewise? A man bowing his knees to the

Father and strengthened by the Father's Spirit, so that Christ dwells in his heart through faith, will surely be "rooted and founded in love". His roots strike down into the rich soil of divine love and he draws thence invigoration for his whole moral being. He is learning that "The Father loves the Son, and has given all things to be in his hand", John 3:35. He learns the greatness of that anointed One who will give effect to all the Father's thoughts. In this way we "may be fully able to apprehend with all the saints what is the breadth and length and depth and height" (verse 18). If the One who is the Centre and Head of God's universe of bliss dwells in our hearts we shall be able to apprehend the blessed character of the whole system. The Father is going to put the impress of Christ upon everything and Christ will fill all things with the light and love of God. The vast expanse of creation will be filled with the effulgence of God. What a triumphant issue of all the ways of God! Well may we be lost in the contemplation of it!

"And to know the love of the Christ which surpasses knowledge" (verse 19). This is a far wider thought than His love to us, blessed as that is. It is the deep devoted love in which He has taken up all the Father's counsels and will give full effect to them for the Father's glory. We miss a great deal of the fulness of Scripture by attaching things so much to ourselves. The Father would have us to see the wonderful place that Christ holds in relation to a 'vast universe of bliss', and how He will pervade it all with His own love, so that it may be filled with what answers perfectly to the Father. The love of Christ will extend to the utmost bounds of the universe of bliss.

We need not be afraid of losing anything by seeing the vastness of this. It serves to enhance our appreciation of our own - that is, the assembly's - peculiar place of nearness and union, for we are His body, "the fulness of him who fills all in all", Ephesians 1:23. It is through the assembly that all that Christ is finds expression. It will need the universe of bliss to show what the assembly is as the fulness of Christ. Then we are His bride, the peculiar, unique and glorious object of His love, presented to Himself for the satisfaction and delight of His heart.

Then Paul would have us "filled even to all the fulness of God" (verse 19). The assembly is the vessel in which God's fulness will be displayed throughout all ages. The vessel is being formed and filled now, and will come out resplendent with divine glory to set forth the fulness of God in a reconciled universe. How little do we take in these wondrous thoughts! The assembly is the fulness of Christ to fill the universe with what is delightful to God, so that He may have rest and complacency in all things. And the assembly is the vessel in which the fulness of God will shine forth, filling all things with light and love and blessedness. We are being filled now in view of all this. There is no less measure for us than the fulness of Christ and of God. How blessed to be receiving of that fulness! We may feel how very small we are to receive, but we are expanded and enlarged by receiving. In natural things the more you put into a vessel the less room there is for more, but in divine things the more the vessel receives the greater its capacity becomes to receive more. And, remember, the Father is "able to do far exceedingly above all which we ask or think, according to the power which works in us". Now is the time to receive the fulness; in another day all that is received will be displayed, and there will be unto God "glory in the assembly in Christ Jesus unto all generations of the age of ages. Amen".

———————

Reading at Teignmouth

9 June 1924

Ephesians 3:14-21; Revelation 21:1-4

Ques.   Is not promise the outcome of purpose?

C.A.C.   Promise has rather to do, generally speaking, with conditions of evil; God's answer to this is the vindication of Himself in regard to it all. He makes His glory to appear in complete victory over all that has been brought in by the power of Satan. This can be measured by the intelligent creature, as we see in Revelation 21:15-17, but when we touch purpose we touch what is immeasurable. There are no measurements of the city in the eternal state; it can be measured by the creature as coming down in the world to come, but when we see it coming down in the eternal state it is not measured - and for a good reason, because it is the tabernacle of God. God is all in all, and what creature could measure that? The city in the world to come is the wonderful product of the activity of God in relation to certain conditions; but in connection with His eternal purpose there are no conditions. It is what God thought of for the satisfaction of His own love when He had nothing to consider but that love. There was no sin or death, neither innocent nor fallen man then, nothing but Christ, the Man of eternal purpose, so there were no limitations - all was immeasurable. In Ephesians 3 it is purpose; we get the breadth, length, depth and height, no measurements but an intimate expanse of blessedness, all of God and according to the greatness of God.

Ques. What is the difference between measure and comprehension?

C.A.C. It is apprehend, not comprehend (see New Translation). It is quite impossible for the creature to comprehend what we have in Ephesians 3, but it may be apprehended by those strengthened by the Father's Spirit; we can apprehend a blessedness that we cannot comprehend. We sing sometimes, 'Tis too vast to comprehend', but it is not too vast to apprehend. We apprehend as strengthened by the Spirit of the Father; the moment you touch that you are outside limitations. It says, "God gives not the Spirit by measure" (John 3:34); when we take account of what comes in by the Spirit we are outside measurements; we are in touch with what is eternal and therefore immeasurable. That is the difference between the city in the world to come and in the eternal state - one is measurable and the other is not. In the eternal state there are no measurements and the city takes the character of the tabernacle of God. We get another dimension in Ephesians 3; in Revelation 21 the city has three dimensions only, breadth, length and height but in Ephesians 3 there is a fourth dimension, depth. That word "depth" connects the whole subject with the eternal purpose of God.

Ques. What is the thought of depth?

C.A.C. I connect it with 1 Corinthians 2:7-10, "But we speak God's wisdom in a mystery, that hidden wisdom which God had predetermined before the ages for our glory: which none of the princes of this age knew, (for had they known, they would not have crucified the Lord of glory;) but according as it is written, Things which eye has not seen, and ear not heard, and which have not come into man's heart, which God has prepared for them that love him, but God has revealed to us by his Spirit; for the Spirit searches all things, even the depths of God". Everybody can see that that is immeasurable.

One feels in reading the two scriptures before us that we have a different conception in them. There is a range of things that can be measured, connected with the administration of the world to come, and it terminates. But there is another aspect of things where there is no limit; it is immeasurable and connected with what is eternal. We belong to, and constitute part of that eternal and immeasurable system. The satisfaction of God is there; it is what God proposed to Himself when there was no man to consider but Christ. In eternity the only Man present in the divine mind was Christ, the Man of eternal purpose, and in that purpose all is according to the measure of Christ and the measure of the Father's love and that is immeasurable. It is important for us to see that the Spirit being a divine Person connects us with what is eternal and immeasurable. At the end of John 3 it says, "God gives not the Spirit by measure", then there is immediately added, "The Father loves the Son, and has given all things to be in his hand". The "all things" are the immeasurable system connected with the Father's love for the Son, and the Spirit connects us with it.

Ques. Would you connect that with Romans 8:39?

C.A.C. Romans 8 brings in the whole expanse of the created universe, "Nor height, nor depth, nor any other creature". It is the whole expanse of the created universe from the height of heaven to the depths of hell, and not a thing in the universe can separate us from the love of God which is in Christ Jesus our Lord. Does it not set you up in triumph? If you had every power of the created universe against you, it is measurable, but you are linked up with the love of God in Christ and that is immeasurable. The measurable things can never disconnect you from what is eternal and immeasurable. The glorious greatness of God begins to shine on one's spirit. It is written that on one occasion, "All were astonished at the glorious greatness of God", Luke 9:43. I believe that is the kind of impression God would leave on our hearts today.

Ques. Do the promises refer to the millennium and purposes to the eternal state?

C.A.C. Yes, the promises will all be fulfilled in the millennium. Eternal life is the summing up of all the promises; it is the distinctive promise. But in purpose you are brought to sonship, and that is the expression of what is immeasurable. In a sense you can measure eternal life, but you cannot measure sonship.

Ques. In the eternal state there is no trace of what is connected with the entrance of sin; it seems to be obliterated.

C.A.C. In the world to come there are

kings and nations, and a large substratum of material not responsive to God, for we see that after the city has been light to the world for a thousand years there is rebellion in the four quarters of the earth, but when you come to what is eternal there is no flaw. Administration in the world to come is perfect, but the conditions in which it is exercised will not be absolutely perfect even in the millennium. We even get a distinct intimation that things will decline among the people of God. There will be no departure from Christ, but there will be a measure of decline. We see that in the diminishing number of the sacrifices through the seven days of the feast of tabernacles which is typical of the world to come - there is a bullock less each day, beginning at thirteen and coming down to seven. That indicates a diminishing apprehension of Christ, and that is the root of decline. But we do not get anything like that in what is eternal, all there has its roots in the depths of God. The administration of the city is perfect but it is a measured administration; in the eternal aspect of the city the thought of measurement is not introduced. Our proper privilege is to look at what belongs to the world to come from the standpoint of sons, of those who have their part in what is eternal; we have an eternal place with Him who is above.

Eternal life is connected with promise; you could not have anything greater on the line of promise than the reversal of everything that is evil and the substitution of all that is blessed and of God. Eternal life in the Old Testament is the blessing, and in the New Testament it is the promise. God committed Himself to man in promise, for as the power of evil showed itself, God met it by promises. He pledged Himself to meet every manifestation of the power of evil by corresponding good. When a man gets to the blessedness of that good, that is eternal life. In answer to every sign of evil that appeared God made a suggestion of Christ. In the Old Testament we see the development of evil which culminated in the rejection of Christ and we see God pledging Himself at every step to meet it, and to bring in a good which stands in relation to the evil but which exceeds it, like the "much rather" in Romans 5:9,10; Romans 5:15; Romans 5:17. We get the whole scope of what came in by Adam and then all that came in by the last Adam, and that brings in eternal life. Romans 5 ends with grace reigning through righteousness to eternal life through Jesus Christ our Lord. That is the gathering up of all the promises; they are connected with all that God committed Himself to in the presence of the power of evil.

But the world of purpose was in the depths of God from eternity, and we cannot fathom it. It was in the depths of God before time; before man or sin were there, there was that which God cherished for His own delight, His own eternal purpose in Christ Jesus. What belongs to eternity has now begun, as we sometimes sing, 'Eternity's begun'. And there will be that which is eternal through the millennium. The saints in the city will not be deprived of what is eternal; they will exercise their administration in the light of what they are as sons. Now in Ephesians 1:3 - 6 we read, "Blessed be the God and Father of our Lord Jesus Christ, who has blessed us with every spiritual blessing in the heavenlies in Christ; according as he has chosen us in him before the world's foundation, that we should be holy and blameless before him in love; having marked us out beforehand for adoption through Jesus Christ to himself, according to the good pleasure of his will, to the praise of the glory of his grace, wherein he has taken us into favour in the Beloved". Who can fathom that? We have got into the depths of God. If we want to understand the depths we have to take account of the wisdom which was foreordained for our glory before the ages. God chose us in Christ and His great desire was to dwell with holy sons - that was His eternal thought. The answer to that is in the opening verses of Revelation 21, the tabernacle of God where He dwells according to His eternal thought in eternity. In connection with the earth God desired to dwell in Zion, and He cherished it - "Here will I dwell, for I have desired it", Psalm 132:14. As to the earth His dwelling is in Zion, but in relation to eternity He desired to dwell in a company of holy sons; they are the ones of whom the Lord spoke, "The men whom thou gavest me", John 17:6.

We are much limited by making ourselves a centre. We shall never be spiritually right until God becomes our centre, because God is the great Head of the universe. "The Christ is the head of every man, but woman's head is the man, and the Christ's head God", 1 Corinthians 11:3. We do not come to the proper centre or head until we come to God. David knew God in His headship; he says, "Thou art exalted as Head above all; and riches and glory are of thee" and so on (1 Chronicles 29:10-19). If we got to that it would be a spring in our souls. In the eternal state God is all in all; everything disappears but God's eternal thought. Think of the blessed God desiring to dwell in a company of holy sons! He has made us holy sons in order to dwell in us eternally. The greatest thought of all is that God should have the satisfaction of His love. In principle God delights to dwell with us now in the character of holy sons: it is the Father's desire, the thought did not originate with us.

The mountain of His inheritance is the fulfilment of His promises to Israel, but being brought to the abode of His holiness is a hint of what is eternal. God had before Him a holy Son, His beloved One. Christ was in God's purpose from eternity: He was not actually Man until He came to earth, born of the virgin, but He was Man in purpose, and God chose us in His holy Son that we should be holy and blameless before Him in love. He would dwell in a company of holy sons. Christ was the beloved from eternity. He was in purpose the beloved holy Son in Manhood, and we were chosen in Him before the world's foundation that we should be holy and blameless in sonship's place, accepted in the Beloved. It is immeasurable! No creature with a golden reed could measure that.

Ques.   What is the thought of chosen?

C.A.C.   I think it is the sovereignty of the God and Father of our Lord Jesus Christ, a sovereign action by which certain persons are elected. The election of God is a personal election. I would have nothing to do with the idea of abstract election. Scripture speaks of names from the foundation of the world - that shows it is individual. Also we get, "Whom he has foreknown, he has also predestinated ... whom he has predestinated, these also he has called; and whom he has called, these also he has justified; but whom he has justified, these also he has glorified", Romans 8:29, 30. No one could question that the calling is personal and individual, or that justifying is personal and individual, and therefore foreknowledge and predestination are personal and individual. If you say, Why did God choose me instead of a million others? I could only bow my head and say with reverence, Because He chose to do so. In eternal purpose God was free to do what His love would have Him do. It is wonderful that in the depths of God every one of that company of holy sons had his distinctive place by name - God's elect before the foundation of the world. After sin had come in and all the ruin of the first creation it was necessary that God should call and justify.

Rem.   People disagree over the subject of sovereignty.

C.A.C.   I think none of us gets right with God until we accept the truth of His sovereignty. The sense of the absolute sovereignty of His mercy and His love puts us right with Him and makes us worshippers. Jacob is the only one in Hebrews 11 who is spoken of as a worshipper, and in him the principle of sovereignty came out in the fullest degree - "I have loved Jacob, and I have hated Esau", Romans 9:13. This is connected with the depths of God in eternity: He was entitled to satisfy His own love.

Ques.   What are the riches of His glory?

C.A.C.   The riches of His glory are connected with the saints being strengthened with the Father's Spirit in the inner man, so that Christ might dwell in our hearts through faith, "In order that ye may be fully able to apprehend with all the saints what is the breadth and length and depth and height". The riches of His glory are something for us to understand now; they are the measure of our present endowment. The Spirit is not often spoken of as the Spirit of the Father; I think this is the only place. What riches of glory it is to have the Father's Spirit! It enables us, as strengthened by the Father's Spirit, to be rooted and founded in love: we get the blessed sense of love. Love is the spring of everything, and then we can apprehend with all saints the breadth, length, depth and height.

Ques.   How does the next word or two come in, "To know the love of the Christ"?

C.A.C.   I think that is to give us a sense

of the height. Only one divine Person can make known Another. The love of Christ is the love of the Head, and Christ is Head of every family. In this great system which has breadth and length and depth and height without measure, Christ is Head of every family, and His love is going to be the mainspring of response to the blessed God in every family eternally. That is what the love of Christ is, it is a provision for an adequate response to the love of God.

In chapter 2 we see how God's quickening power wrought, where there was nothing but depth, in order to bring us to the heavenlies in holy sonship; that is the length. The divine working in the souls of His saints is a long process. The quickening of chapter 2 has been going on for nearly two thousand years and it will result in a quickened company of holy sons who will be a dwelling place for God in eternity. Then there is the height. Nothing is so high as the love of the Father for the Son; none of us will ever know what that is. We cannot understand the love of the Father for the Son in Deity - that is beyond the creature - but we can know the love of the Father to the Son in manhood for He prayed that "the love with which thou hast loved me may be in them", John 17:26. That is the height, and He prayed that it might be in us. Then there is another side, response.

There is nothing so high as the responsive love of Christ to the Father, the responsive love of the Head to bring every family to respond to the Father; that is height.

'Suited to Thine own thoughts above, As sons like Him, with Him to be'. That is eternal and immeasurable.

Ques. Is it love to the Father?

C.A.C. I think it is the love of the Head; He is the wonderful Head of this immeasurable system characterised by breadth, length, depth and height, created in the purpose of God and brought to pass in the power of the Spirit. Every part of this system is under the influence of a glorious Head who is characterised by surpassing love. "To know the love of the Christ which surpasses knowledge"; that is immeasurable. Paul wants us to know it, so that we might answer to the keynote struck by the Head. The love of Christ is the spring that will make every part of the universe of bliss vibrate in response to the Father's love throughout the eternal day. It will fill every heart to overflowing. There you are lost; the apostle does not attempt to describe it. He prays that we may "apprehend with all the saints what is the breadth and length and depth and height", but he says nothing of measurement. The blessedness of God in His nature brought into the universe in purpose is infinite. It is amazing that we should form part of that wonderful city which comes down in the eternal state - no measurements there, but a vessel capable of being filled to all the fulness of God, that God may dwell in His company of holy sons. He will have a people on earth who know Him, but He will dwell in a tabernacle comprised of holy sons. Heaven is learning today, "principalities and authorities in the heavenlies" are learning, through the assembly "the all-various wisdom of God"; that is the breadth, and He will display in the assembly "in the coming ages the surpassing riches of his grace", Ephesians 2:7. He is teaching angels today, and He will show it to men in the new earth in eternity. Angels are called sons of God, and so they are interested in what God is doing; there could not be holy sons uninterested in what God is doing. The angels form an outer circle, but they are intensely interested in those who form the inner circle. See how they came forth and could not hold their peace when that blessed One came into this world, God with us, a pledge of all the promises: "A multitude of the heavenly host, praising God and saying, Glory to God in the highest, and on earth peace, good pleasure in men", Luke 2:13, 14. They rejoiced in what God was doing in getting another company of holy sons from among men.

The effect of rightly apprehending all this would be that we should be beside ourselves to God. How do we get into it? If we had the apostle Paul here - in a sense we are listening to him - he could not help us further. He could only set these things before us to move our spirits, to fire our hearts with holy devotion but he could not give it to us; we must bow our knees to the God and Father of our Lord Jesus Christ that it may be reached in our souls. It is essential that we should bow our knees to the Father to have granted to us this wonderful strengthening by the Spirit, so that we should have the consciousness, and not merely be able to sing, that 'Eternity's begun'. We can touch what is eternal as holy sons.

In the presence of every kind of evil, sickness and death, the greatness of Christ came out. He cleansed the leper; a person died, He could bring him to life; He gave sight to the blind. And His moral perfections - what a wonderful contrast to every other man! He grew up before Jehovah as a tender plant: He is spoken of in many passages as a sprout, which suggests a shoot of an entirely different character from anything else seen. He grew up in all the perfection and beauty of holy

Manhood, delightful to God in the midst of evil. There was that about the Lord to which nothing in the natural man answered, as we read in Isaiah 53, they saw "no form nor lordliness" in Him; that is the right word. Think of the lordliness of Christ! The Supper is the lordly Supper! What distinctiveness and surpassing excellence, what dignity and lordliness were seen in Christ in the midst of all that was evil here! He was the root out of the dry ground. But when we get to the eternal thoughts we see the delight of the Father in His Beloved in circumstances and conditions that are congenial to the Father's love. Here He was for a moment, a visitation of divine perfection passing through this dark world! John looked on Jesus "as he walked". He was moving from the sacrificial position which sin had made a necessity to His abiding place; and John writes so that we might move from what is temporal to what is abiding and eternal. In following Christ we pass from what is connected with sin and death to His abiding position. The two disciples said, "Where abidest thou?" And they came and "abode with him that day", John 1:38, 39. It was the abiding place of the Son in Manhood, and He is saying today, "Come and see". May the Lord help us to meditate on these things, first of all to see the blessedness of the city that can be measured, and then the blessedness of that which cannot be measured but which abides eternally, the dwelling place of God in the company of holy sons.

When God has glorified Himself in relation to all that has come in, then He will rest in His love according to His eternal purpose.

Rem.   There is a peculiar freshness about all this - the city coming down as a bride in the eternal state suggests freshness.

C.A.C. Yes, it suggests the thought that the peculiar fervency of bridal affections will never be dimmed throughout eternity. The city in the eternal state will have all the freshness of bridal attire and affection which will never wane; that is what she will be in relation to Christ. The assembly will stand eternally in relation to Christ and will never lose the bloom of bridal affection. In ordinary cases you do not speak of a bride after a person has been married a few years, but in the divine thought the bride continues for eternity in the freshness and bloom of first affection. Christ will be the true Adam and in the bride adorned for her husband we see the true Eve. God's primary thoughts are eternal.

———————

Reading at Teignmouth
28 August 1923
Ephesians 4:8-16

C.A.C   How very important it is for us that we should have the Lord before our hearts as the ascended One. I have no doubt that we all accept as a fact that He has ascended, but one would desire to have a greater impression on one's heart of Christ as ascended. It is not the same thought as we get at the end of chapter 1, where we read of the mighty power of God which raised Him from the dead, and "set him down at his right hand ... above every principality, and authority, and power, and dominion"; that is not at all the same as His ascension. In chapter 1 it is what God did with the One whom He raised from the dead; He set Him at His own right hand: that is what God did. But the ascending is what Christ did. That is the difference between the way it is presented in Mark and Luke, and the way it is presented in John. In Mark we are told He was taken up, and in Luke we are told He was carried up. In Acts 1 He was taken up, and in Luke 9 we read about the days of His receiving up, but in John He says, "I ascend" (chapter 20: 17): it is not what is done with Him. "I ascend" is in the majestic dignity of His own Person, just as His rising in John 2:19 is in the dignity and power of His Person. It is not God raising Him; He says, "I will raise it up"; it brings out the dignity of His Person as the Son of God. I think it is of immense moment to see this. When He ascended it is what He did Himself; it is His triumphal return from the accomplishment of the mighty victory which has changed everything for God and man.

Ques.   Why does it say, "Wherefore he says"?

C.A.C.   It is referring to the testimony of the holy Scriptures, (Psalm 68). In that Psalm it is God's victory; the Psalm begins, "Let God arise, let his enemies be scattered". It is God's victory, but when we come to the New Testament we see that God's victory is accomplished in a Man. That is very precious; it is a Man who has led captivity captive, and that is the very One who could go up in His own dignity and power.

I have thought a good bit lately of His death as it is presented in John, "I lay down my life". John's gospel brings out the dignity and glory of His Person as the Son of God: as the Son of God He ascends triumphantly. In the beginning of Hebrews we read He "set himself down" (chapter 1: 3). It is the greatness of the Son there, One who could make purgation of sins and set Himself down. It is all accomplished in a Man; it is God's mighty victory over all His enemies, but it is accomplished in a Man, and the results of it are for men. One feels the importance of not passing over it in a cursory kind of way.

Ques. Does that give character to the gifts?

C.A.C. Yes, I think so, because the gifts show how the victory becomes known and its fruits available. We see the mighty Victor returning from the battlefield carrying, as it were, all the spoils of victory. He has led captivity captive and the question is, if He has gained such a victory for man, how is the fruit of it going to be known and enjoyed? Well, it is through the gifts. We do not see the power of Satan and all his hosts overthrown publicly; they are not overthrown in relation to the world, but they are overthrown in relation to Christ. As that Person is before us we are in the good of the divine victory. What a blessed thing, in the midst of a scene where evil predominates on all hands, to be able to look up and see the victorious Christ; He has gone above all heavens, above every created position, however glorious.

Rem. The next part of verse 10 leads to what is future.

C.A.C. Yes, I think so; He is going to dispossess everything else; that is the result of His descending into the lower parts of the earth. He is going to be the theme of every tongue. It is a wonderful thought that all is to be filled by that blessed Man, and if He is going to fill all things presently, He is able to fill them now. The body is the first thing to be filled. There is that on this earth now that stands in relation to the One who has ascended up above all heavens, His body, and that body is the first vessel to be filled.

It is very blessed that the thought of His ascending suggests the thought of His descent, and that He has gone to the utmost limit of the enemy's power. He has gone to the lower parts of the earth; it is lower than Philippians 2. He has linked the two extremities, i.e., the summit of His glory and the lower parts of the earth. It was not sufficient that He should go to death, the death of the cross. The obedient One goes to death, even the death of the cross and He is highly exalted. That is the path of the obedient One to accomplish the will of God, and He is highly exalted. But here He has descended - going to the full extent of the enemy's power.

Ques. Would that be connected with the enemy's overthrow?

C.A.C. I think it is so. In Matthew the Lord speaks of being in the heart of the earth. He not only goes to death - it is a blessed thing that He goes to death - but He goes farther. He lies three days and three nights in the heart of the earth, and He dispossesses the enemy of all his weapons: He leads captive all the power of the enemy. Every evil power has become the witness of the victorious power of Christ.

Rem. That, I suppose, is connected with His having led captivity captive.

C.A.C. Yes, the moment you look at the power of evil in relation to Christ you see how completely everything has been subjugated. Satan's power is here, death is here; everything is in moral confusion. The important thing is that the ascended One should fill our souls. The gifts are all in the power of that. How should we know about the victory of Christ so as to be in the gain and value of it but for the gifts? None of us here would know anything about the ascended One if He had not given gifts: it is through the gifts that He has been made known for nearly two thousand years. The prowess of Christ has been made known in that way.

Ques. Will you open that out a bit?

C.A.C. Well, we should not have known

anything about the victory of Christ if He had not given gifts, if there had not been apostles and prophets. All that we have in the New Testament Scriptures is through the exercise of the gifts of the ascended Christ. The gospels and the epistles were written by men who were the gifts of the ascended Christ, and they have made known to us His victory and how every power of evil is completely subjugated if looked at in connection with Christ. The apostles and prophets are the foundation, but what the apostles taught has been handed on. What Paul said to Timothy he was to pass on to others, and in that way the wonderful account of Christ reaches down.

Ques.   Would it be right to say that the gifts with which the assembly is endowed will last as long as the assembly is here?

C.A.C.   Yes, I think so. The persons are the gifts. They are not like gifts deposited in a man with which the man is not in accord; it is what the man is that constitutes the gift.

Rem.   I suppose it would not be of much value otherwise.

C.A.C.   No. I think it is the impression of Christ made on a man that tells. One would like to have a more profound sense of being livingly connected with Christ in heaven.

The twelve apostles were sent by the Lord

in the days of His flesh. They were men amongst whom the Lord had gone in and out in the days of His flesh, and who were specially witnesses of His resurrection. Peter says, 'There must be twelve witnesses of His resurrection, and they must be men who had been with the Lord from the days of John the baptist until He was taken up'. The witness-bearing of the twelve concerns all that transpired from the ministry of John the baptist until the day that the Lord was taken up. I daresay many of us stand a little in the good of that ministry, the witness-bearing of what Christ was in the days of His flesh and as risen. What we get here is another thing, the ascended One gives gifts; they come down from a glorified Christ in heaven, and they are connected with the body here.

Ques. Would Paul be a good illustration of what was received from the ascended One?

C.A.C. I thought so. Paul presents in a very distinctive way the character of the gifts that come from Christ ascended.

Ques. With regard to the lower parts of the earth, was it there that the members of the body were formed? Psalm 139:15 says, "When I was made in secret, curiously wrought in the lower parts of the earth".

C.A.C. I think everything was disclosed at

the lowest point that was necessary to form the members.

Ques. Did I understand correctly that you said the lower parts of the earth refer directly to the burial of Christ?

C.A.C. I think it does. The Lord Himself speaks of the Son of Man being three days and three nights in the heart of the earth. When Paul speaks of the gospel he insists upon what is often left out by preachers: "That Christ died for our sins, according to the scriptures; and that he was buried; and that he was raised the third day, according to the scriptures", 1 Corinthians 15:3, 4. Paul makes His burial an essential point. In connection with the gospel it involves the complete disappearance of all that for which He went into death sacrificially; it is buried; it is not only that He died but He was buried. So Christians are buried with Him; it is good for us to learn what this means. It means that we are to disappear as to any place or importance that we might have thought attached to us as men in the flesh, that we might come into view in another character in newness of life.

Rem. The lower parts of the earth are brought in here as the utmost limits of the enemy's domain.

C.A.C. I thought so. He must go to the

extreme limit of the enemy's power. He must come down from the summit of divine glory and go to the lowest depths. The result is that as to all the powers of evil they are just a horde of captives dispossessed, only remaining as trophies of His victory; He goes back triumphant, and that is how we know Him. We know Him far above all heavens.

The evangelist goes out that the triumphs of Christ may be made known, "even for the rebellious, for the dwelling there of Jah Elohim", Psalm 68:18. It has been said that what we see in Christ is God's thought for men accomplished. The evangelist's mission is universal. The work of the evangelist is to bring in men, and then that they may be built up. The gifts are for the perfecting of the saints, for the work of the ministry, for the edifying of the body of Christ. It is that which is in view.

The apostles and prophets are clearly the foundation, chapter 2 makes that plain: "Ye are fellow-citizens of the saints, and of the household of God, being built upon the foundation of the apostles and prophets" (verses 19, 20). The apostles and prophets are foundation: stones and we have their ministry in the Scriptures so that everything now must be substantiated by Scripture. The Lord may still in sovereignty give gifts that are of apostolic character - men sent with a distinctive mission to the whole church, like Luther. There have been times of great crisis in the church, and men have been raised up with a distinct mission. In the fourth century God raised up Athanasius and gave him a distinct mission, and the truth of the deity of Christ was re-established, and there have been other instances in the history of the assembly when men have been found whose service had such a universal and special bearing that the gift seemed to partake of apostolic character. Of course such men have had to prove everything from Scripture; they had not apostolic authority or inspiration. I am only referring to the special character and scope of their mission. They were given in the power of the ascended Christ to establish some great truth for the assembly that had been lost sight of.

Ques.   So has the truth been unfolded and maintained in that way up to the present time?

C.A.C.   I think so. The Lord has not failed to raise up men who have been distinctive gifts from Himself in heaven.

Rem.   You would not hesitate to say that J. N. D. was an apostle.

C.A.C.   I believe he was distinctly sent to

restore the truth of the headship of Christ and what stands vitally connected with it; and that his mission was universal in its scope, an apostle in that sense, if you like.

Ques. Have we not rather confined apostleship to the twelve?

C.A.C. I think we get in the twelve what marks apostleship in the principle of it. With the bringing in of the apostle Paul there was a distinct movement in the unfolding of the truth; and it is by the gifts of the ascended Christ that His victory and its fruits are made known so that the saints may be perfected and spiritual service carried on, so that the body of Christ may be edified with a certain object in view. How it all brings before us the love and faithfulness of the One who has ascended above all the heavens! I do not suppose that any of these gifts have been withdrawn; they were given to operate "until we all arrive at the unity of the faith and of the knowledge of the Son of God ...". It is very blessed to note what is in view.

Ques. What do you mean by the reference to prophetic ministry?

C.A.C. Things were communicated to the saints at the beginning by prophetic gifts as well as by apostolic gifts. There were prophets in the assembly by whom revelations were given. The assembly was founded upon the ministry of the apostles and prophets; the mind of God was declared in that way.

Speaking of the edifying of the body, it says, "until we all arrive at the unity of the faith and of the knowledge of the Son of God, at the full-grown man, at the measure of the stature of the fulness of the Christ". That is what is in view, and if that blessed end were reached there would be no need for the exercise of the gifts any longer; the body would be capable of edifying itself without gifts. It is the end that is in view but we have not arrived at it yet.

Ques.   Is there anything in the order in which these gifts are given here?

C.A.C.   I thought that the foundation gifts came first, and then evangelistic gifts to make Christ known in the world in His victorious power, and then the shepherds and teachers to care for those who have believed.

Ques.   What are prophets?

C.A.C.   I thought it referred to those by whom the mind of God was revealed in the early days. It is very comforting that nothing has been lost; we have the inspired record in the Scriptures of what the apostles and prophets made known. It is there for the body of Christ still, and that body is also the vessel of the Holy Spirit. However great the power of evil may be, even in the church, divine activities are still going on "until we all arrive at the unity of the faith ...". (verse 13). The faith would include all that God has made known; the whole system of divine truth would be summed up in the faith. The centre of it all is the Son of God. The edifying of the body of Christ is going on in spite of all the inroads of the enemy at the present time. It is most touching to consider the character of the gospel of John. John was kept in reserve until the ruin of the church was fully manifested and then at nearly one hundred years of age he sits down to write a gospel. One would have thought that an apostle writing in such conditions would have a great deal to say about failure and ruin: he does not say a word about it! He writes about the Son of God; that is the kind of ministry for the day of ruin. He brings in a glorious Person who is unchanged and unchangeable, and he sets before us the blessed possibility of having life in His name. God would not have us fretting our souls about evil. The evil is there and it is right to feel it, but God would have us on the line of life in the name of His Son.

Ques. Would you mind continuing the thought of what there is for us to arrive at?

C.A.C.   The result of arriving at the unity of the faith and the knowledge of the Son of God would be that we should arrive at the full-grown man. The saints collectively would be adequate to express the stature of the fulness of the Christ. It is the whole company of saints, the body, brought to be adequate to express the stature of the fulness of the Christ; the assembly will be seen as "the fulness of him who fills all in all" (chapter 1: 23). The gifts are all working with a view to bringing that about now, bringing it about morally. It will be brought about eventually by divine power so that collectively there will be an expression of Christ. That is the divine mind. But this scripture evidently has in view its being reached now, because it goes on to show what the results will be, that we should be no longer babes, that we should not be led about by evil teaching and systematized error. The saints, as having been brought up to the measure of the stature of the fulness of the Christ would not be carried away by winds of doctrine, "but, holding the truth in love" would "grow up to him in all things, who is the head, the Christ".

Rem.   I think you have said that there were gifts given that are not available.

C.A.C.   Well, it should be an exercise with

us all, if we have anything that is given for the body, that it should be put into circulation. Every saint has an impression of Christ, but I think there is a great power of Satan at work amongst us to hinder the communication of what is divinely precious. Instead of communicating what we are enjoying of Christ we are often diverted to talk of odds and ends that are of no encouragement or help to anybody. It is necessary to pay attention to the gifts which have been conferred. It speaks here of every joint supplying something; "each one part" is to supply something.

That is "first works". The Lord says to Ephesus, "Repent, and do the first works". For every joint and every band and each part to be supplying something for the encouragement and building up of the body would be "first works", which go along with "first love".

Reading at Teignmouth

1932

Ephesians 5:1-33

C.A.C.   It may be well to go over briefly the line of truth that has been before us in these readings on the body. We began by seeing that in Romans great prominence is given to the Spirit; as the Spirit has place with us the body comes into expression; it becomes manifest that the saints are one body in Christ. That prepares us for Corinthians where we find the Spirit assigns to different members different functions. The fact that they all function in unity and co-ordinate without human arrangement brings the body into eminence. Then we saw that as the body comes in it makes room for the Head; that is the moral order. The recognition of the Spirit brings in the body and the body being in evidence makes room for the Head as in Colossians. Then there is no limit to the possibilities of entrance into the revealed mind of God. The resources are unlimited; therefore the saints move on to Ephesians where we see the climax of the subject.

On the last occasion we looked at Ephesians where we see the body in its eternal aspect, the fulness of Him that fills all in all. It brings in a new thought which it is very necessary we should apprehend spiritually, that is the thought of Christ as Head, as the Husband. He is Head in the most blessed character in which the headship of Christ is known by the assembly. That is what is developed in Ephesians 5.

Ques.   Would that take us back to Eve derived from Adam?

C.A.C.   We should have some difficulty in understanding how the wife is the body and the body is the wife if we had not Eve to help us. Both aspects are linked together in this chapter, which it is important to understand. The leading thought in the chapter is the husband and wife, but then the wife is the body, too, and the type elucidates it for us. We see that Eve was brought to Adam - that is union. The assembly is viewed in Ephesians as brought to union. Eve was Adam's wife, but she was the body, too, she was himself.

Ques.   In Revelation we get the marriage of the Lamb. Is there union previous to that?

C.A.C.   Yes, Ephesians does not give you the bride, it carries you to the thought of the wife. The wife is a more extended thought than the bride.

Ques.   There is a reference to the husband

in Revelation 21 in relation to the church as a bride adorned for her husband. Would you say a word as to that?

C.A.C.   It is used by way of comparison. The bride has lost none of the freshness, beauty or ornament of her bridal state. The bride is also the wife in Revelation. The body and the wife will subsist for eternity. The body as here in the scene of Christ's rejection is to represent the moral features that came out in Christ here, but when she is seen as the fulness of Him that filleth all in all, she is not seen in the features which marked Him here but the features of the heavenly Man who fills the universe of bliss. Whatever quality there is in the bride, it merges into the relation of the wife.

Ques.   It was not the bride with Eve?

C.A.C.   That thought does not come in because she is a divine formation; she is brought to Adam and there is union. When you think of the wife you get the thought of union; the bride suggests freshness and ornament of the initial stage. The bride will be for display in the millennial day, she loses nothing in a thousand years, she is still as a bride; she has that character and freshness; there is no sign of decay or going off.

Ques.   Would you say a word as to how the

body functions?

C.A.C.   The body is the fulness of Him that fills all in all. The fulness is adequate to set forth all that is in Him. The assembly as the body is adequate to set forth all that belongs to Christ in conditions of glory. We do not know much about that; we know something about Christ as humbled here and His body as having the traits of Christ humbled here, but of the other side we know little.

Christ as Head is the perfect setting forth of what God is morally; that is very prominent in Ephesians. The Spirit is charged with the ministry of this to us but we do not know much about that side. We can all, thank God, appreciate the humbled Christ and appreciate His lowly features, but think of the glorious heavenly Man in His own surroundings and glory - it is a wonderful thing! Nothing would move us more than Ephesians 5 where we see the personal love of Christ to the assembly. He is Head to the assembly in the sense of being Husband; then there comes out the wonderful character of the Husband. He loved the assembly and gave Himself for it. We have that verse before us every Lord's day morning but we do not know much about it.

Ques.   What does it convey?

C.A.C.   I suppose it sets forth the length to

which His love is prepared to go; there is no thought of atonement or redemption in it. The intensity and persistence and measure of His love is so great. It is sacrificial at the beginning of the chapter, "Walk in love, even as the Christ loved us, and delivered himself up for us, an offering and sacrifice to God for a sweet-smelling savour" (chapter 5: 2); that is sacrificial but I doubt if there is any such thought in the delivering up of Christ for the assembly. The death of Christ is viewed in this peculiar aspect that God is not brought into it; if you bring God in you bring in the sacrificial idea, but this aspect is Christ and the assembly, and Christ's love for the assembly. He gave Himself, not to redeem it but to sanctify and purify it. It is the movements of Christ in love that He may have the assembly. He must leave His father and mother in order that He might get the assembly. In Ephesians 5 it is the movements of Isaac; it is the man who moves in Ephesians 5; he leaves father and mother for his wife. In order to get the assembly Christ had to move, to leave father and mother representing Israel and the whole system of things connected with Israel, which had a great hold on His affections. It cost Him something to give that up in order to get the assembly. He left Israel and the promises and all connected in the mind of

God with Israel; He left it by way of death because He could not have the assembly otherwise. How that should affect the wife!

Rem.   It should draw out our affections.

C.A.C.   There is a hymn which just expresses it:

"By love constrained, Thy death we deem
Our point of severance from this scene
    Where man Thy rights did spurn;
To us earth stands in shadow now,
(For Thou art absent), until Thou,
    Lord Jesus, shalt return."

Miss F.J.Elwood

That is the delivering up of Christ for the assembly in the sense of Ephesians 5.

Ques.   Would it bring in the thought that the assembly was to be subject entirely?

C.A.C.   Yes, a subjection to the Head as known in love and the experience of union. We do not know much about it. The assembly is subjected to Christ; she is put into that position; it is the experience of union that brings her to it. This subjection is only known by those who are in union. We all know subjection to Christ as Lord; there are certain things due to Him; His commandments are to be obeyed; but it is a different thing to be united to Him in the bonds of love of which His death is the eternal witness. It is a beautiful conception and a precious divine reality. We should pray that it may be a reality experimentally to us. There was no voluntary action on the part of Adam; God put him to sleep. You could not have this thought in Ephesians 5 in type.

Ques. Is union different from united to a unity?

C.A.C. There is unity in the body here but union is the assembly brought in affection to Christ in glory now, in the conscious power of being in union with Him there. The Spirit emphasises in Ephesians the movements of Christ. He went through death and severed links with Israel in order to have the assembly and now He purifies it by the washing of water by the word so that sin is not in view at all. The Lord is continually bringing this washing of water by the word to bear on us. His death has severed all His links with Israel and the promises in order that He might have the assembly; there is not a question of sin or faults or blemishes.

Ques. Is having the assembly glorious the answer to the way He moved?

C.A.C. Yes, the assembly is to be morally glorious, perfectly suited for union with the heavenly Man. "Spot" (verse 27) does not refer to sin but is something not heavenly. The assembly is not to have a thing out of keeping with the gloried Man; it is a question of being purified from everything connected with earth in order to be in union with a glorified Man in heaven. A "wrinkle" means that we are not so bright as we once were. The Lord's love will not have anything like that. If some of us here are not as bright as we were a few years back, that is a wrinkle; the Lord cannot tolerate that in His wife, it would show that she is declining. There was not a feature lacking in Eve that could appeal to the affections of a man; that is how the assembly is to be to Christ. There will be no sanctifying or washing or purifying in heaven; that is going on now. The idea is that the assembly should be morally glorious now. We will not talk of being holy and without blame in heaven; the fact that the assembly is to be holy and without blame is that she is to be looked at thus in relation to conditions now. Think of persons being in this world without a spot on them, suited to be united to a heavenly Man! It is too great for us; it is stupendous! I think it is brought about by this peculiar yielding to the precious service of Christ. It is not Lordship but a yielding to the known love of One with whom you are in conscious union; that is what makes it easy to yield.

In verses 28, 29 and 30, we come to the link between the thought of the wife and the body. That is, no one ever hated his own flesh and men ought to love their wives as their own bodies. Now the thought is brought in of the body. This is the highest thought of the body; we have come to the climax. The thought of the body does not belong to any other family; it is the only thing that is distinctive to the assembly. It is a great thing to think of His own flesh; that is the thought of the body. I have been interested in tracing out the thought of His own flesh as developed in John's gospel. I would earnestly ask the brethren to look at John's gospel in the light of the assembly being His own flesh. It begins with the thought of the saints as born of God; that is how John gets at it. If the saints are not born of God they are nothing that Christ could regard as His own flesh. Chapter 17 says twice over, "They are not of the world, as I am not of the world"; that is His own flesh. We have often heard that John supports Paul; he does not use Paul's language but he gets you there. Then we get the thought of the saints as born of God; they are of Christ's fulness, and that which is born of the Spirit is spirit - that is near the thought of His own flesh. Then we get, "He that practises the truth comes to the light" (John 3:21) - that is His own flesh. All His works are wrought in God, and all that practise the truth, their works are wrought in God. In John 4, those who worship, worship in spirit and truth; they have that character, they are morally Christ's flesh; that is what He loves and gave Himself for. In chapter 13 He looks at the saints as loving in the same way that He loved: that is His own flesh; if I can love as Christ loves, I am of His flesh. The saints in John are brought into correspondence with Him, they are His own flesh. They are equal in affection and can be intelligent as Christ is: "For all things which I have heard of my Father I have made known to you", John 15:15. He gave them the capacity to understand what the Father said to Him. We used to be told that nothing could be united to Christ that did not come from Him. The assembly is Christ's own flesh; it is wonderful to think of it! Paul said, "This mystery is great". He could also say, "But in that I now live in flesh, I live by faith, the faith of the Son of God, who has loved me and given himself for me", Galatians 2:20. He walked in the light of the Person he ministered.

Two Readings at Teignmouth

From notes taken

Ephesians 5:22-33

The setting of this scripture would suggest that it requires the highest degree of spirituality to take it up. It supposes and requires that the saints shall be filled with the Spirit. As filled with the Spirit there are conditions in which they can realise the gain of the headship of Christ. This section is particularly based on that, there is no movement of the flesh; any movement of the flesh would surely hinder.

"Submitting yourselves to one another in the fear of Christ" means that Christ is owned in the saints, that is, we submit ourselves to one another on that principle, that Christ is in them. So that one would like to move in a spirit of submission to the brethren as owning Christ in them; one would be afraid of doing anything that ran counter to any feeling or thought of the brethren generally, looking at them as having Christ in them. You look for faith and love for Christ in the assembly and for Christ in the saints; that is how faith and love regards them. So that anything out of line with the mind and feelings of the brethren is to be avoided because Christ is in them. There cannot be any cleavage when there is submission, and practically it is the only thing that will save us. We are to be subject, not only to God but to the brethren as animated by Christ; He is vitally in them. That is why we pay great respect to the saints. We are tested in a way by them; that is the test. Some might say, Well, the saints may be wrong! But that is upsetting the whole thing; you have lost all sense of Christ in them. The general sense of the saints is not wrong; it is much more likely that they are in the mind of Christ than that I am when I am indifferent to them.

And is it not as Head that the Lord becomes Saviour? "Saviour of the body" is an oft-discussed scripture, and it finds its solution in seeing that Christ is Head of the assembly and that it is in that character that He is Saviour of the body. That is, it is as coming under headship that there is salvation, whether as to the individual body of the saint or in the extended view of it in the assembly. The salvation comes in in the recognition of the headship of Christ. It is salvation on a positive line, not the keeping from evil; lordship does that but Christ's blessed headship serves the assembly positively, and it is as entirely shutting out the whole principle of self and the movements of our own wills. Here it is not exactly as in Romans, which is on the line of lordship, but on the line of headship which works in affection and brings about submission on the line of love, a very happy condition. It is an oft-discussed passage; I think the Spirit of God has purposely left it as of very wide application. We want the spirit of it, the reality of it, then everything will be right.

That the assembly is subjected to Christ is a permanent position. The assembly stands in a definite relationship; we are not looked at as moving according to flesh but according to Christ. The assembly that He loves is the assembly that stands in this relationship to Him, not a company of half-converted people! We ought to know the touch of it in assembly. When we have broken bread together and reach in a spiritual way the thought of Christ's headship, and the relation of the assembly to Him as Head, we should look for His direction to be realised. We sometimes lose our way in the service of the assembly but the recognition of Christ in His headship would preserve us from any uncertainty in our movements. We have little idea of what Christ as Head could be to a wholly spiritual company. That the assembly is subjected to Christ is the fixed position. So it is with wives in relation to husbands; the thing is put absolutely, there is no qualification with it; wives are to obey always, not only when the husband is right. When a woman is married she comes into a certain fixed relation which nothing can change; nothing is optional. The relation of the assembly to Christ is the same. When Eve was brought to Adam it was a divinely determined relationship with which nothing was to interfere. How the assembly is subjected to Christ should be learnt in the assembly, in that sphere, and so it is to be worked out in our relationships. You cannot think of a wife going against her husband in anything unless it is a question of disobeying God; then the superior rights come into action. Would this not have a sanctifying effect upon us if we were spiritual enough to appreciate the moral beauty and excellence of it? Then there are conditions in which God can help us, and will help us. It is, I suppose, as having accepted the defined relationship that we learn in verses 25-27 how it works - in Christ. All this underlies headship.

J.T. said some years ago that he thought the Lord saw the assembly in His disciples. It was before Him as a concrete reality in certain persons; He saw it in those persons and loved them. It was not a mere abstract conception that He loved; certain persons were given to Him of the Father and were so attractive that He loved them. I thought it a very happy suggestion. We see particularly in John 17 what they were to Him; and even in the parables in Matthew, the assembly gospel, you get the pearl. It was there; the Lord saw it in the disciples, and it was worthwhile to secure it. We often dwell on the Romans side of His death, "While we were yet sinners, Christ died for us", but the work of God effects in the saints that which is attractive to the Lord. All this brings to us the sense of the intimacy and reality of the love of Christ; with all reverence we can say that Christ could not love what was unlovely. The thing is there in principle. The constitution was there in principle in the disciples who surrounded Him, and in that relation He could serve them by delivering Himself up with that in view, the purifying and washing of water by the word, "that he might present the assembly to himself glorious, having no spot, or wrinkle, or any of such things; but that it might be holy and blameless". If Esther had not been essentially beautiful, all the months of purifying would not have made her so. But it was intended to develop what was there; and so it is with the assembly.

I do not think there is any type in the Old Testament that completely expresses what we get here. What is stated here is so wonderful and unique that it could not find expression fully in any type. It waited for Christ. It was necessary that the Man should appear and that He should be in a condition in which He could have a wife united to Him. It helps if we think of the extraordinary position in which Christ is because He could not have any wife until He was glorified, so that really the assembly is formed out of a glorified Christ. It gives a wonderful thought of the service of the Spirit as having come down from a glorified Christ to form an assembly for eternal union with the wondrous Person from whom He has come. Even the apostle seems at a loss; he says, "This mystery is great". He expresses holy wonder in the contemplation of it.

Now Eve did not need any sanctifying or purifying so she does not give you in type what you get here. There is a precious service of Christ for the assembly, He "delivered himself up for it"; that is the great underlying fact; His love has gone to the extreme point. But then there is this service going on which seems to be illustrated in the book of Esther: in verse 12 of chapter 2 we read that when every maiden's turn came after the twelve months for purification, six months with oil of myrrh and six months with spices, "whatever she desired was given her to go with her out of the house of the women to the king's house". It is a beautiful illustration of it, six months with oil of myrrh speaking of all the fragrance of His suffering love, then six months with spices; and then it is suggested that something depends on her own exercise in desiring things, because whatever she desired was given her. I think that is a beautiful touch, that the Spirit of God contemplates that there will be special desires on the part of the saints composing the assembly that "whatever she desired was given her". The two go together. The active service of Christ is not without intelligent exercise on the part of the assembly so that there are desires. Whatever she desires is given her. I like that; it gives us something to pray for. This is what is going on at the present time; it is not past history but current history! This is peculiarly the time when this is going on.

I thought that the sanctifying and purifying were brought out here to enhance before us the precious service of Christ. I do not think it is to occupy us exactly with defects on the part of the wife any more than the purifying of the women suggests defects. They were very choice maidens who were selected, and any thought of defect or defilement is not quite suggested. The assembly must necessarily be brought up to this glorious condition to be presented glorious. It is rather the thought of excellence and beauty conferred than defilement removed. The process in Esther is not to make an ugly woman beautiful or a defiled person clean; the idea of such to be queen would not enter into it, but a superlative excellence was to be conferred. If we are to be united to a glorified Man, what must be the standard of beauty and preparedness and fitness? But it is all looked at as the service of love. In John 17 the Lord says, "I sanctify myself for them, that they also may be sanctified by truth" (verse 19), and that is after He has told the Father twice, "They are not of the world, as I am not of the world", John 17:14, 16. Think of Him repeating it, saying it twice to the Father!

As to the type one cannot doubt for a moment that Adam was the most perfect man that ever stood on earth, and it is equally true that Eve was the most perfect woman - the workmanship of God. He built her. It suggests a most skilful workmanship on God's part. And she answered most perfectly to Adam, there was not anything lacking. Well, that is what the assembly is to Christ. We were saying that the most exalted degree of spirituality is needed to understand this passage, because it follows immediately on being filled with the Spirit which is necessary to take it in. Still, that does not prevent us from having a peep at it; we should never read anything if we were up to it before contemplating it! It is difficult for us to take in the thought of being formed out of Christ as Eve was out of Adam. The formation of Eve out of Adam is without question the most extraordinary thing that God ever did. He could give extension in an extraordinary way. If we can take it in, God has before Him a blessed Man who has been through death and resurrection, and who is now glorified; and God can take what is purely of that glorified Man and give it extension in the assembly, so that when the moment comes for presentation there will not be anything there but what came out of Christ. You might say, 'I cannot understand it!' Well, it is God's thought; He says, 'That is what I am going to do'.

All moral excellence enters into this. "Holy and blameless" would suggest the completeness of the assembly morally. When Eve was formed out of Adam he was an innocent man, moral features were not there; he did not know good from evil. But Christ, out of whom the assembly is formed, is One in whom every moral question has been developed and glorified, and so she must have corresponding moral features. Christ loved righteousness and hated iniquity and it is in that character that He has companions, as we see in Hebrews; so the assembly will be marked eternally by these features.

When we come to the divine side of things, God has instituted the marriage relation to convey thoughts that we could not have entered into without the relation, that is, the family relation and the relation of husband and wife. God has provided a suitable setting in human affairs to illustrate His wonderful thoughts; we could not have taken them in otherwise. The thought of husband and wife is introduced of necessity first, and then consequent on that you get the family thought. Satan's object is always to darken the divine thought. He is always working to bring in conditions contrary to God's mind, so that the husband and wife do not always get on well together; the children are often disobedient to their parents, and that darkens the divine thought. The world would be justified in mocking at the testimony of such. But the divine thought is that these great matters connected with the assembly should come into spiritual reality; it is the time of the formation of the assembly. I suppose it would be, and often is, realised after we have broken bread together. The Lord shows how He has delivered Himself up for us, and under the influence of that we should understand there is this washing of water by the word and sanctifying; that is, the Lord would bring something before us as together that would displace natural and human thoughts and fill us with a sense of what the assembly is to Him.

I think we should be exercised that there ought to be ministry from the Lord when we are in assembly. We do not often get a word from the Lord - I state it as a fact - and we are missing something. We should look for the service of the Lord in this way. It must be due to a want of looking to the Lord to apply the word, this "washing of water by the word", so that all human and natural thoughts might be washed away and we are left under the pure and holy influence of the word of the Christ. "Let the word of the Christ dwell in you richly, in all wisdom teaching and admonishing one another", Colossians 3:16. It comes in in that connection. Perhaps sometimes we think that what we say to the Lord is more important than what He says to us. There is an extraordinary sense of self-importance in that. What we could say to the Lord could never come up to what He could say to us. There is nothing whatever said here of the service of the assembly to the Lord.

Reading at Hedge End, Hants,
5 May 1936
Ephesians 5:25-30; John 15:9-12

C.A.C. It was on my heart that we might consider a little the love of Christ to the assembly as His wife, and that we might see the measure and character of that love and what it has in view. Then I thought we might see how it is worked out in pattern in a company of men in this world in the gospel of John. For John has a great place in the wisdom of God as filling out and developing what has been presented by Paul.

Ques. Is the relationship of wife to be known by the saints now?

C.A.C. I thought that the assembly is the wife before she is the bride. The bride is more for display, but the wife is for the satisfaction of the husband. And Christ is serving the assembly in His unlimited love with a view to a complete result. The thought of perfection is being reached in the object of His love - she is to be completely satisfactory to His own heart.

Ques. Is that what is developed in verse 32 - a great mystery?

C.A.C. Yes, the natural relationship of husband and wife is introduced, but only to bring out what is connected with Christ and the assembly. We see the extreme devotion of Christ to the assembly: He delivered Himself up for her. That is not the thought of atonement. When it is a question of dealing with sin, the action is that of God; God delivered Him up for us all, and it was Jehovah who made his soul an offering for sin. But He delivered Himself up by His own act and with a view to a complete result; she will be satisfactory in every way to His own heart. "Christ ... delivered Himself up" is a statement that occurs only three times in Scripture. It occurs in Galatians 2:20 where Paul says, "The Son of God, who has loved me and given himself for me"; it is the same word. It also occurs in verse 2 of this chapter, "Christ ... delivered himself up for us, an offering and sacrifice to God for a sweet-smelling savour", and it occurs here in relation to the assembly. It is the unreserved devotion of His love and His thoughts and service toward us at this moment are according to the love in which He delivered Himself up for us.

Ques. Is the sanctifying and washing the present service?

C.A.C. Yes, it is, but it is the thought of a

completed result. We have been looking at the prominence in Scripture of the thought of a complete result. We were looking at it in connection with the kingdom; "first the blade, then an ear, then full corn in the ear", Mark 4:28. A complete mature result is secured on earth, not in heaven but on earth in the kingdom. And when the complete result is reached He puts in the sickle. The washing of water by the word is adequate means to bring about a completed result; and I would suggest that it is set forth in pattern in the men that we see in the gospel of John. The completed result was there so that they were morally quite suitable to be with Him in glory and to see His glory.

It is rather remarkable that in Scripture when it is a question of making ready for the marriage it says, "His wife has made herself ready", Revelation 19:7. There is a moral force in that; it is the exercises of the wife, and all that has come out in her as the wife in the place of responsibility, that have made the wedding garments, because it is the righteousnesses of the saints. She appears as the bride in the value of all that she has acquired as the wife. There is a certain intimacy about a wife that there is not in a bride. A bride is one newly come to the position, but a wife is matured in her appreciation of her husband and in her affections and in her knowledge of his mind; if you could think of a perfect husband and a perfect wife, she would come up to the full measure of his thoughts. That is the idea in Ephesians 5; the assembly, through the washing of water by the word is to come up to the full measure of His thoughts so that He can present her "to himself glorious, having no spot, or wrinkle, or any of such things"; she is "holy and blameless".

Ques.   Is it a similar thought to "The heart of her husband confideth in her", Proverbs 31:11?

C.A.C.   Yes, she is the worthy recipient of his confidence. If you read what the Lord says about these men in John 17 you will see He says nothing about a spot or wrinkle or any such thing. He has in His mind and before His heart a washed and purified company in whom there is neither spot or wrinkle or any such thing, but which is holy and blameless; He can commit all His interests to them. It is a mature result; they are men. Now I think the Lord would exercise us as to whether we have really apprehended the thought of His love to secure a mature result morally now so that we fill the place of wife in a way that is completely satisfactory to the heart of Christ.

Rem.   He says, "Ye are already clean",

John 15:3.

C.A.C. That indicates to us the wonderful power of the word by which He washes us. I think we sometimes get the idea that this washing goes on piecemeal; a little bit cleansed here and another little bit cleansed there and a good deal of imperfection left. But that is not the Lord's idea of washing at all, for He says, "He that is washed all over needs not to wash save his feet, but is wholly clean", John 13:10. Is not that a complete result?

Ques. Is the wife always ready to be presented?

C.A.C. I think the divine conception is that the assembly should be at any moment suitable for presentation; and is not there a presentation every Lord's day morning? If the Lord comes to us there is a certain presentation of the assembly in a spiritual way now.

Ques. When the Lord speaks of giving Himself, is that the complete thought?

C.A.C. It was a complete dedication of Himself in the self-sacrifice of love. The same word is used of Barnabas and Paul. The assembly at Jerusalem commended them as men that had "given up their lives", Acts 15:26. It is the same word. It is devotion that knows no limit and no reserve. I think we see in the gospel of John, particularly in chapters 13 to 17, that which in this world was His own flesh. It was not strange or alien to Him. He says, "They are not of the world, as I am not of the world", John 17:16.

Ques.   Does Adam give the idea, "bone of my bones" Genesis 2:23?

C.A.C.   Yes, she is his counterpart. If the assembly is the counterpart of Christ, that is the complete result. This washing of water by the word is very important, because I am afraid we often think of it as if it were a service that deals with what is objectionable in the saints piecemeal, a bit at a time, but I do not think that is the idea. It effects a complete result at once, so that as the Lord sat down at the supper table, He was surrounded by a cleansed and purified company. Not all of them, I admit, because Judas was there, but the company as a whole was clean; the complete result had been reached. Think of what the word is, the washing of water by the word, it is the blessed testimony of the Father communicated by the Son and that communication is essentially pure and holy. It makes no account whatever of the world, or of the natural man or of the man after the flesh. It makes everything of what God is and of what He has secured in Christ. Now it was that powerful testimony of what was in Christ that cleansed them, and it had brought a new element into their souls that had no taint or blemish upon it. In the view of the Lord that characterised them. What they had received had been applied to them by the washing of water by the word and that characterised them.

Ques.   Would that be the way in which He could say, "As the Father has loved me, I also have loved you", John 15:9?

C.A.C.   That is very beautiful and it helps very much because that is the love of complacency. If He loved them as the Father loved Him, He was able to view them without "spot, or wrinkle, or any of such things".

Ques.   Is it the thought of presentation in chapter 17, "be with me where I am"?

C.A.C.   There is no disparity, they can be introduced into a scene of glory where the Father is glorified in the Son and all the Father's purposes and counsels are brought to fruition without the slightest taint of disparity or unsuitability. To really enjoy our place with the Lord and with God in the assembly we need to apprehend that; that is partly why I suggested it, because if there is not the sense of this complete cleansing by that which has been brought to us through the word, we shall not be thoroughly at home with divine Persons. The word that He had spoken to them brought in entirely new elements. It was not a modification of the natural, or an improvement of it or something added to it; it is entirely new elements. The Father is revealed in the Son and the Son expresses the Father and delivers Himself up so that everything connected with sin and defilement might pass out of sight. In this gospel the Lord is seen bearing His cross and going forth to the place of a skull. What an end of all that man is! His great thoughts and pride and everything else - what are they in the place of a skull? And in John's gospel there is a beautiful touch: it says there were two others crucified with Him; it does not say anything about their character or the history of their souls, but just the fact that two others were crucified with Him. It is the testimony in these two that there was to be an end of the man after the flesh. Now if that man is ended and all that is of God is brought in and brought to bear upon our souls by the love of Christ, it is a complete cleansing. It is what is entirely new, it is Christ and the Father's love. How pure and holy is a company of persons who are cherishing that! The washing is by the introduction of something altogether and divinely new and perfect and it sets aside by its power, when applied by the love of Christ to the soul, everything that was there before, and elements come in in which Christ can delight, which become suitable for presentation to Himself.

Ques. What would you say as to feet-washing?

C.A.C. That is a very important and necessary question, because the feet-washing shows how the love of Christ considers us in our present position in a scene of defilement. We cannot put our feet down on a spot that has no defilement. Now the Lord considers for the saints, so that we may not be hindered from enjoying this complete purification which His love has brought in. The more we are conscious that we are without "spot, or wrinkle, or any of such things" the more we feel anything which would soil, and the feet-washing comes in in connection with that, so that we may not be distracted from the sense of being perfectly at home with Him.

I suppose the service is continuous, because as long as we are in the scene of defilement we need the service of feet-washing. The Lord has inaugurated it, but He has shown, at the same time, that He has others that can do it. If He can wash feet, they can wash feet; they are His own flesh.

Ques. When is that done?

C.A.C. I suppose it is really a continuous

service which is carried on as we understand the nature of the complete cleansing. We must understand the nature of the complete cleansing in order to be able to do this service which only applies to the feet. It is done in the intercourse of the brethren one with another, and it is done in the meeting, and it is done by the ministry of the word. We have known what it was to be affected by the circumstances we have passed through having lost the sense of entire suitability, but as we come to a meeting there is a cleansing process which bears witness to us of the love of Christ. It is a purled and cleansed company who alone can understand feet-washing. If we do not know the complete purification and cleansing effected by Christ for the assembly we shall not apprehend the feet-washing; we shall not know the character of it. I think it is most important to see that all the elements that have come in, the knowledge of the Father and the knowledge of Christ, have come in through the incarnation of Christ and have no connection with the fallen man whatever; they have come from heaven and are entirely of God. There is no admixture of these things with the fallen man or the fallen state. Think of that passing in cleansing power over our souls by the love of Christ!

Now I wanted to say a little as to the

nourishing and cherishing; I think the Lord would not have these to be vague thoughts to us. The nourishing is the idea of sustaining and support. I believe the Lord sustains and supports and nourishes His wife with that which He has proved to be of the greatest power for sustenance Himself.

Ques.   Do you refer to the verse in John 6:33, "the bread of God", come down from heaven?

C.A.C.   I think it refers particularly to the verse there where the Lord says, "As the living Father has sent me and I live on account of the Father" (verse 57). What a secret support that was! As a Man in this world He lived by the Father. Now I believe that is the character of nourishment that He would minister to His wife. He could say, "My food is that I should do the will of him that has sent me, and that I should finish his work", John 4:34. That was more in connection with His service; He had food in His service in finishing the Father's work - He was sustained and fed. Now that is the character of food which the Lord would in His love make a great reality to us. So that the gospel of John, and particularly these chapters at the supper table, are to be greatly studied in connection with the way that He brings out the Father. There is no greater source of sustenance and strength for the assembly as the wife of Christ than the knowledge of the Father. It is the greatest spiritual nourishment possible. The Father is that particular revelation of God which marks the present time; it is that manifestation of God which has come out through the Son, so that there is a peculiar quality about it. As has often been said, the Father is the name of grace. And the Lord tells us distinctly that His words were the Father's words. Now the love of Christ would bring the nourishing power of the Father's words unto His wife to nourish her, that she might be nourished and strengthened and fortified by all that which is the joy of His own heart. How else could she be suitable to Him? And so, great importance attaches to the Father being brought in very distinctly and blessedly in the assembly, because the strengthening of the assembly as the wife is dependent upon the knowledge of the Father. Not that it is exactly an advanced thought, because John says little children know the Father; but it is a most nourishing thing. Can you think of anything more pure and holy than a person detached from the world and nourished by the words that came from the Son? A complete result, surely!

Then another great point in the nourishing seems to be connected with the presence of the Comforter. I do not know anything more sustaining than the presence of the Comforter. The Lord realised that Himself - the Spirit of God descended and abode upon Him. It was a great support to Him. I say that with reverence and advisedly - it was a great support to that blessed One when the Spirit came down and abode upon Him. There was nothing to disturb the rest of the Holy Spirit in that blessed Person, and He could speak of Himself as the One whom the Father had sealed. It is said, too, that the Father gave Him the Spirit without measure. I suppose that could never be true of any other. But what strength there was in it! What sustainment and support! And so when He speaks of the Comforter coming, it was a Person well known to Himself, in all the blessed support that the Spirit could be to a holy Person down here. Remember, we are talking about holy persons now, who correspond with Christ, who can do as He did and who can love as He did and be hated as He was. It is that holy, sanctified, purled company which constitutes His wife, His assembly. Think of the effect on such a company as that of having the Comforter. One who comes close beside you: that is the idea, that the Holy Spirit comes close to your side. Now the Lord nourishes His wife by bringing these things in continual ministry before us. These things are being woven into the warp and woof of our spiritual being all the time, and constitute our spiritual strength.

Then another source of nourishment would be the sense that we have of immediate access to the Father and the Son. We can ask for anything connected with us as the wife - there is not a single thing that belongs to us as the wife of Christ that we cannot ask for and get immediately. He does not put in any conditions; He says, 'I will do it' and He says the same of the Father, 'He will do it'. I may ask a great deal connected with myself, but that is not the wife. The wife has no interest but His interest, no matters or business of her own; and it is beautiful to think that the Lord has no business but the assembly. The man in Deuteronomy 24 who marries a new wife is exempted from all military duties and all business that he may pay all his attention to his wife and gladden her. How precious to think that Christ at the present time is exempt from all governmental concerns! He is carrying on no warfare, He is giving His undivided attention in love to the assembly.

Then there is the thought of cherishing. That is, by the manifestation of His love He cherishes the proper affections of the assembly as His wife. He knows how to express His love so that He can call upon them in John 15 to love one another as He had loved them. That is, He appeals to the experience they had had of His love. Now it is a poor thing if the Lord cannot appeal to some experience of His love in our hearts. We do not know much of the place of the wife if He cannot appeal to an experience of His love. He says, "As I have loved you". They had experienced it in the feet-washing and therefore I think it is a serving love, love to the brethren that would serve them at personal cost. You can always serve the brethren; you cannot always be complacent in them, perhaps but you can always serve them. But in chapter 15 it is complacent love. What a wonderful thing to hear Him say that the Father's love to Him was the measure and character of His love to them. It shows how entirely they were in His view without spot or wrinkle or any such thing. Now, He says, "Love one another, as I have loved you". All that has been expressed in Christ as the Husband is to come out in the assembly as the wife. I believe the thought of Christ is that the beautiful movements of holy and spiritual affections that make manifest that she is His own flesh should come into expression here in this world before we are in heaven. I believe it is the divine thought that the wife should come into actual expression here in this wonderful activity of holy affections which make it manifest that she is His own flesh. And I think if we study these chapters in John we shall see that the assembly is there, you might say, essentially. John does not give us the assembly formally but He gives us the very substance, the very nature of it. In John 17 the Lord does not ask for the Spirit to be given to them, which is very suggestive, because I believe the Lord was speaking to the Father in the light of the complete result of all that He had done and of His being glorified, and therefore He regards them in His prayer as having the Spirit. He can commit them to the Father as those whom He had guarded and carried through in the fidelity of His love. And now He turns them over to the Father as suitable persons for the Father to keep and to sanctify and finally to place in His own presence in suitability to be there. When the Lord delivered Himself up for the assembly He had seen it in its true spiritual character and value in the men whom the Father had given Him out of the world; He had seen it and He had loved it. The love of Christ is not a sovereign love, it is a discriminating love and a selective love, a love that loves what is lovable. And it is very blessed to see that we have the assembly in John, not formally but vitally and substantially, in a spiritual way.

———————

Word at Teignmouth

1 January 1905
Ephesians 5:25-27

I should like to say a few words on the aspect of the death of Christ which this scripture presents to us. We dwell much, and rightly, on that precious death as the basis of all our blessing and joy. We gladly own that the One who gave Himself to secure every blessing for us is worthy of our endless praise. But let us not forget that He gave Himself for the assembly "that he might sanctify it, purifying it by the washing of water by the word". He gave Himself that His death might become effective in the present sanctification of the assembly.

Coming together to remember the One who has been in death should have an intensely practical effect upon us. There is no moment in our history when the death of Christ is brought nearer to us than when we are together to eat the Lord's supper. We realise how that death has come in to sever us from this world and from all that we are according to the flesh. In this way we come under "washing of water by the word".

But this, if a spiritual reality, must have a

great effect upon us. How can we return to that which we disallow in God's presence? How can we be here to praise the Lord that He has removed man after the flesh before God in holy judgment, and then return to a life in which we allow the flesh and its motives to have place?

The divine effect of coming together to eat the Lord's supper must be to draw us in spirit and affection into more entire and practical separation from all that for and to which He died. Thus the assembly, entering into the love of Christ, is sanctified and cleansed from everything unsuited to that love.

To what extent does this sanctification go? The assembly will be presented to Christ "glorious, having no spot, or wrinkle, or any of such things; but ... holy and blameless"! It may be said that this will never be until she is glorified above; but the point of this scripture is that Christ is sanctifying and purifying the assembly now with the washing of water by the word that she may be morally ready for presentation to Himself in the beauty of holiness. The love of Christ will not suffer anything to remain that is unsuited to itself. He does not shut His eyes to the spots and wrinkles and blemishes, but His love sets itself to remove them. We may tolerate blemishes in ourselves and in one another, but Christ would never tolerate a blemish in the assembly. The assembly will be presented to Christ in glory as the moral result of what He has done in sanctifying and purifying her, and she will be displayed in that glory to His praise. He is working for that now.

If we come together and find it blessed to contemplate the love in which Christ went into death for the assembly, how can we return to the allowance, even in thought or motive, of that which is unsuitable to Christ - that for which He died? He gave Himself for the assembly that He might make His death effective in our present sanctification and purifying "by washing of water by the word". Christ is thus making His bride suitable for presentation to Himself. May we know increasingly this divine effect of coming together to eat the Lord's supper and remember Him!

Reading at Exeter

4 January 1933

Ephesians 5:22-33

C.A.C. It is noticeable that of the nine references to the assembly in this epistle, six of them come in the few verses that we have read, so that it is peculiarly an assembly setting of things that is before us here. And it seems to be worthy of note that what is brought before us in this section is brought out in an affectionate relation. It is rather remarkable that Paul did not bring out the truth of the assembly as the wife in the teaching part of the epistle; he does not bring it out until he comes to address wives and husbands. That is, he puts it in an affectionate setting and brings it out in connection with the most affectionate relations that are known to men.

Ques. In instituting the relationship in the beginning, had God this before Him?

C.A.C. Yes. I have no doubt at all that the original relationship of husband and wife was established in view of the relations that were to subsist between Christ and the assembly. When they were instituted they became an affectionate setting in which the truth of Christ and the assembly could be developed, but the type was not adequate to set forth all that was in the thought of God. On the part of Adam there was not any self-devotion in love nor any intelligent service of love towards Eve. The type was there but like all other types it was only a shadow; it was not the very image of the thing. Types are precious and exceedingly helpful but for the very image of the thing we have to come to Christ and to the assembly. There is a difference between a shadow and an image; a man's shadow on the wall does not give you his features; it gives you an outline and that is what we should look for in a type, the outline. The New Testament gives the filling out, the very image. There is a great deal in Ephesians 5 that we get no intimation of in Genesis 2.

Ques.   Do you get it in any of the other types?

C.A.C.   I do not know that you do. There are different types of the assembly; certain women of old represent the assembly in different features, but there is a surpassing fulness and preciousness in this chapter. One feels the need of a spiritual atmosphere for the consideration of such a scripture. Paul had said much of the assembly in the course of his different epistles, but it is not until this chapter that he speaks of her as the wife.

Ques. Is this view of the assembly particularly connected with eternity?

C.A.C. Well, it is eternal because the great thought is what the assembly is for Christ, and this is peculiarly precious. Paul dwells much more on the truth of the body than he does on the truth of the wife, and I suppose that is necessary. The great thought in the body is derivation - the body derives from Christ. Eve derived from Adam in a way that is not set forth in any other type; she was taken out of Adam. That is more the idea of the body; the assembly, as the body, is derived from Christ; it comes out of Him and it could not really be for Him if it did not come from Him. But then, after Eve was taken out of Adam she was brought to him; now that is Ephesians 5. Chapter 4 teaches that the body derives from Him: "Holding the truth in love, we may grow up to him in all things, who is the head, the Christ: from whom the whole body, fitted together, and connected by every joint of supply, according to the working in its measure of each one part, works for itself the increase of the body to its self-building up in love" (verses 15-17). All there derives from Him, but here (chapter 5) the thought is that the assembly as the wife is secured for Christ.

She is for Him in the sense that He is free to carry on all the service of His love towards her, so that in result she may be everything that His heart desires for its complete satisfaction. It is a wonderful thought.

Ques.   Is that producing fruit for Christ?

C.A.C.   Well, the thought hardly comes in Ephesians 5. It is the thought of the service of His love towards her, and what she becomes for His satisfaction. It ends in His presenting the assembly to Himself glorious, without "spot, or wrinkle, or any of such things ... holy and blameless"; she is absolutely perfected for His satisfaction.

Rem.   And she is like Himself.

C.A.C.   Yes, His counterpart. Eve was the counterpart of Adam, and the assembly is destined to be the counterpart of Christ.

Rem.   The unspiritual could not understand why the apostle kept this wonderful truth until the close.

C.A.C.   He kept it back because it is the crown of everything. J.B.S. used to tell us that the climax of things was union; now that is what we get in this chapter, it is the only place in Paul's teaching where the assembly is seen as the wife.

The aspect of the Lord's death here is very precious, and it is all the more precious because it does not say in so many words that He died for the assembly. What is before us here is not what He has accomplished in the way of purgation or reconciliation or the glorifying of God in death; all that, of course, was true, but there is something in a sense greater than that, and that is the devotion in which He was prepared to deliver Himself up. In the intelligent action of His love He gave Himself entirely over to whatever might be involved in what He had undertaken to bring about.

Ques.   Does the thought of the Hebrew servant come in?

C.A.C.   Yes, in connection with service. If you think of the Lord's death as the supreme service of His love, which it was, there is the type there. The Lord perfectly understood the value of what He was delivering up when He delivered up Himself. He gave Himself up to whatever might be involved in securing what His heart was set upon. Whatever was involved in, or necessitated by that path of love on which He had entered, He delivered Himself up. It brings out the amazing value of what He devoted in love.

Ques.   How this would enhance the value of the assembly! Would the climax be presenting it to Himself?

C.A.C.   Yes, if such preciousness and value

and infinite worth has been delivered up for the assembly, there must be an adequate answer. The adequate answer is that He gets the assembly and has the joy of serving it in love until it becomes the perfect reflex of every thought of beauty that is in His own heart.

Ques.　Does the apostle refer to this when he speaks of "the fulness of him who fills all in all"?

C.A.C.　I thought we saw at the end of chapter 1 the universal headship of Christ, and in that universal headship the assembly stands in relation to Him as His fulness. The fulness of the Head is expressed in the assembly in a way that will never come out in any other company of saints. He is Head over all things to the assembly, and she is His fulness; she stands in relation to Him in His universal glory as His fulness; that is there will be a shining out in the assembly of His fulness. The king's wife is linked with him; however great the glory of his kingdom and the extent of his dominions, when he goes about in his royal visitations the queen is by his side and is seen to share all with him.

Rem.　Paul speaks of "a light above the brightness of the sun", Acts 26:13. The sun had paled in comparison, so the type in

Genesis pales in the presence of what we have here.

C.A.C.   Yes. You feel, after all, that is only the shadow, and now you are in the presence of the glorious substance. Adam is the great type of Christ as Head and, in a certain sense, he is a figure of Christ as Head over all things, for all the created domain was under Adam and Eve was his fulness. She was his counterpart; the features that came out in Adam could come out in her; there was no disparity between them.

The work of God is to prepare us to be influenced by Christ. A great point in this epistle is that He has been set at God's right hand, and He is there according to Psalm 19; the heavens have become a tent, or tabernacle for the bridegroom. In that Psalm we read that "The heavens declare the glory of God", and the supreme glory of the heavens is the sun. God has set a tabernacle for the sun; "He is as a bridegroom going forth from his chamber" and He goes through the whole circuit of the heavens, "and there is nothing hid from the heat thereof". There is a supreme and commanding influence in heaven at this moment, and that influence is the influence of Christ as the Bridegroom. Shining down from the heavens of the divine glory are beams that shine from the

Bridegroom and the work of God makes us sensitive to the influence of that light. We have in this chapter, "Wake up, thou that sleepest, and arise up from among the dead, and the Christ shall shine upon thee". The result of Christ shining upon us is that we come under the influence of His love. It is the influence of the Bridegroom whose tabernacle at the present moment is in the heavens and who is moving over the whole appointed course until every soul that has been chosen of God to be part of His wife comes under the shining and influence of what is emanating from Him in heaven; that is how the assembly as the wife is formed. She is formed under the influence of the love of the heavenly Christ.

Ques.   Do you connect all that with the thought of derivation?

C.A.C.   This is how the assembly is brought to Him, not how she draws from Him. Chapter 4 opens out how she derives from Him, just as Eve derived from Adam. But it was another side of things when Jehovah brought her to Adam, and that is the idea here, that the assembly is brought to Christ. The result of coming under His influence by the work of God is that the assembly is brought to Christ and she is subjected to Him; that is the point.

Ques. Do I understand that the assembly existed before Christ loved her?

C.A.C. Well, she is presented as being in view of the mind and heart of Christ; all that the assembly was to be for His satisfaction was present to His heart and mind, so that in His love He devoted Himself for her. He delivered Himself over to everything that was needed to make the assembly His own.

Rem. I suppose we have to take in one thought at a time; the derivation has to be looked at at one time and this at another.

C.A.C. Yes. The thought of the body and the wife blend ultimately, but we can look at them separately. As the body, all derives from Christ. As the wife, all is for Christ, subjected to Christ. This precious section is full of the activity of the love of Christ. We are told that Christ is Head of the assembly and that she is subjected to Him, and after that all is His activity in love.

Ques. Is it the love of Christ that has brought that subjection about?

C.A.C. Yes, and the work of God prepares us to be influenced by the love of Christ, by the warmth of it. That is a wonderful word in Psalm 19, "There is nothing hid from the heat thereof"; not only the light thereof, but the heat thereof. The heat speaks of the love of Christ, but none of us would have been influenced by the love of Christ apart from the work of God; the work of God makes us impressionable to the love of Christ and then we come into the place of being subjected to Christ. The assembly is subjected to Christ; she is not merely to be obedient to Him, but to be the subject of the service of His love, for what we find here is that He does everything. He does much more than Adam ever did for Eve.

Ques.   Is the thought of sanctifying and purifying the present activity of His love?

C.A.C.   Yes, the assembly is subjected to Him in the sense that she becomes the subject of His service. It is most important that, through the work of God, she should be subject to the service of His love. He would carry it on; He delivered Himself up in order that He might do so.

Ques.   Does that limit the thought to the assembly?

C.A.C.   It is limited to the assembly clearly. Christ is Head of the assembly here. It has been said, and I think it is quite true, that "the assembly" is a very exalted designation, because it implies intelligence, and Christ can stand in marital relation to the assembly. Adam could not stand in marital relation to any of the creatures that were there for there was disparity; there was no counterpart for Adam. Now, the assembly is a company formed through divine working to be intelligently and affectionately the counterpart of Christ, so that He can stand in marital relation: He can be her Husband - to that company, and that company can be to Him all that a wife should be for such a Husband. Very wonderful!

Ques. Is this work of Christ going on during the sin period, and does it cease at His coming when the assembly is translated?

C.A.C. Well, I think the divine thought is that it finishes before the assembly is translated, because the point is that the assembly as the fruit of the service of love and the purifying of love becomes all that He wants her to be before she is translated. She is to be presented "to himself glorious, having no spot, or wrinkle, or any of such things", as the result of His purifying service, not as the result of His translating power. Her suitability to Him is brought about morally and affectionately. Christ serves her in love so that the assembly may have this character of holiness and blamelessness and everything that answers to His pleasure before she is translated. He delivered Himself up for the assembly in order that He might sanctify it. The Christ, the Head, would have us apart from every impression that does not come to us from Himself and through His own death. There is that in Himself, particularly in His delivering Himself up for us, that is sufficient to set us apart from every other influence. Then there is purifying by the washing of water by the word; there is a moral process carried on. The blessed character and import of Christ delivering Himself up for us is brought home in purifying power by ministry in the assembly. I do not know whether I am right but I have an impression that this is properly the character of assembly ministry.

Ques. What do you mean by assembly ministry?

C.A.C. Well, ministry when the saints are convened in assembly. I believe there has been a great disregard of the love of Christ in regard of that. There should be liberty for this purifying service to be carried on through ministry in the assembly, that which would have the character of direct service of the Head towards the assembly, in the character of the wife. I feel that if we were more awake to that we should get peculiar touches from the Head when we are together in assembly. We must not think that what we can say to the Lord or even to the Father is the greatest thing in the assembly; a word from the Head would surely take precedence of all else in the assembly. I am sure that if the Lord actually came into our midst in a visible way, we should wait to hear what He would say. We should not be in a great hurry to speak to Him; we should all feel instinctively that there was something better than that we should speak to Him and that is that He should speak to us. That must be greater. I think we suffer from the fact that in bygone days there used to be too much of what I might call sermonising in the morning on levitical lines. Men able to minister give a word pretty much as they might at any other time, but in the assembly should we not look for ministry that is in a special way from the Head? So that it is not merely that a brother gives a word, but there is something which we can recognise as from the Head, Christ's service of love bringing the purifying influence of the delivering up of Christ, and all its import in purifying power to our affections. What a precious thing it would be. The scripture before us tonight suggests that there is such a thing as the purifying of the assembly, the saints viewed in assembly character.

Ques.　Would it flow out of the breaking of bread?

C.A.C.　There is no time more favourable for the service of Christ as Head in love than the meeting for the breaking of bread. I wonder whether we have left enough room for the service of the Head; that is the question.

Rem.   It should be a great concern for us all to feel that the Lord speaking to us is greater than our speaking to Him, and it would make us all desire that there should be room for the Lord to speak. When He did, it would carry conviction that it was from the Lord and it would have the effect of bringing in this holy element.

C.A.C.   Yes, and it would result in worship. You may be sure that Christ as Head would never say so much that there was no room for response. If the Head ministered to us, it would be with a view to bring us into line with Himself so that He might carry us with Him into the presence of His God and Father.

Ques.   Do you connect the word from the Head with ministry particularly, or might it not come through a hymn?

C.A.C.   A hymn is evidently addressed by us to the Lord or to God; it is our speaking to divine Persons.

Ques.   We speak of calling Him into presence. Do you not think if we really knew what that was that we should get this word from the Head?

C.A.C. I think so, and its purifying efficacy would be known, so that all that is unsuitable in His wife would be got rid of. The purifying goes on until the assembly becomes suitable for presentation to Himself. It is brought to that point morally before being actually translated. It is very great; one feels how little one has entered into it.

Rem. In the Revelation it says, "His wife has made herself ready".

C.A.C. I think the Revelation largely presents things from the responsible side, and hence we find that His wife has made herself ready. It has been said, and I believe it is right, that it regards the saints as having passed the judgment seat. At the judgment seat everything will be adjusted; all the things that have not been adjusted before will be adjusted then, and she has made herself ready. "It was given to her that she should be clothed in fine linen, bright and pure; for the fine linen is the righteousnesses of the saints", Revelation 19:8. She is seen there adorned in a wedding garment that has been made stitch by stitch through moving on spiritual lines in the responsible course here. But things are looked at in Ephesians 5 entirely from the side of the service of Christ, and to get the benefit of this there is only one thing necessary, and that is subjection. The only feature mentioned of the assembly is that she is subjected to the Christ. The feature of subjection makes room for all His service of love and its results, and Paul's adding, "He is Saviour of the body", shows how practical it all is. He looks at the body of a sister (because it is sisters he is speaking to) as being a subject vessel. Now Christ as Head of the assembly is "Saviour of the body"; He looks at the body as a subject vessel. There may be an intimation in it of the body in a spiritual sense also, but I believe it refers to the actual body. It is in the bodies of the saints that the spirit of subjection comes out; it is not something up in the air but a very practical thing, and the saving power of the Head is vouchsafed to every subject vessel. It is a comfort to know that as part of the wife we have not to be concerned about active service but about the spirit of subjection. Having said that Christ is the Head of the assembly, Paul says, in a kind of parenthesis, "He is Saviour of the body". The assembly is committed to subjection; we are assured of support and preservation for every subject vessel. If we want His support, we must see to it that our bodies are vessels of subjection, then the precious service of the love of Christ can go on.

It is very striking that the assembly is not

said to do anything in this chapter. He does everything. He loves, He delivers Himself up, He sanctifies, He purifies, He presents, He nourishes and cherishes; it is all the service of His love. That is Headship: we get His universal Headship in chapter 1, His Headship of the body in chapter 4 and derivation of everything from Him, and now we get His Headship of the assembly, an intelligent company marked by subjection, a company that is subject to Christ for His service in love to bring the most precious and divine influences to bear upon them. He delivered Himself up in order that He might be able to do it. We have just to be subject; that is the place of the wife, the place of the assembly, subjection. That is what we want to be more exercised about.

———

Reading at Exeter

11 January 1933

Ephesians 5

C.A.C. There would seem to be a very precious thought suggested to us as to the constitution of the assembly when it is referred to as Christ's own flesh; there is a thought of what one might call spiritual substance there. "No one has ever hated his own flesh, but nourishes and cherishes it, even as also the Christ the assembly". It is His own flesh. There was an interesting question asked last week that we did not go into particularly as to whether the assembly was in existence before Christ loved it. I think it would be right to say that it was.

Ques. Do you mean in purpose?

C.A.C. I was not thinking of purpose but substance, for in the thought of the assembly being His own flesh, we have the thought of substance in a spiritual sense.

Ques. Would Psalm 139 support that?

C.A.C. The thought is suggested there of the formation of spiritual substance; it has in view the fashioning of the members of Christ, which is looked at as a prolonged process: "During many days were they fashioned". The members are all written in the book, that is in purpose, but the members of Christ have been fashioned by a spiritual process that has gone on now for nearly two thousand years. But it is interesting to see that the substance of the assembly was there before Christ loved it and delivered Himself up for it.

Ques.   Is your thought that the merchant man in Matthew 13:46, having found one pearl of great price, sold all that he had and bought it?

C.A.C.   That is the idea; it was there.

Ques.   I thought the servant was sent to find the wife (Genesis 24). It is not exactly the seeking of Christ. Do you not get the Isaac type here rather than the Adam type, because it is in the sin period?

C.A.C. That is true, but it is rather remarkable that the service of the Spirit does not appear at all in this chapter.

Rem.   I thought His work was done, that the assembly was complete and presented to Christ, as Rebecca was presented to Isaac.

C.A.C.   Yes, but that is the end in view; it is not all reached in Ephesians 5. He has not yet presented the assembly to Himself glorious. We are on the way to that consummation.

The service of His love which is active to secure that end is going on, and I think it is essential to the passage to see that the whole subject of it is the devotion of Christ and the service of His love, which does not come out either in Adam or Isaac. There is that in this chapter which finds no place in the typical presentation. It is a reserved glory which does not find a place in either of those types. What we have here is the action of Christ in the devotion of His love, though, of course, we well know that whatever He does, He does by the Spirit.

Rem.   My thought was that this work of Christ is not to produce the assembly, but in order that He might sanctify it and purify it in a defiling scene.

C.A.C.   Yes, that is just the point that we have before us at the moment, that the substance of the assembly was there to be loved and that Christ delivered Himself up for it; He serves it unweariedly until everything is accomplished that His heart desires. He has in view that it shall be reached spiritually before the moment of translation. The presentation to Himself is the result of His purifying and cleansing and nourishing and cherishing; it is the result of a spiritual process and not brought about by an act of power. The translation of the assembly will be an act of power, but what is presented to us here is Christ's service of love and certain things effectuated by that service. The Spirit does not appear in the scene; it is all the action of Christ. Our thoughts are concentrated upon what Christ does and a service of which we have no real type. There is no type in the Old Testament which fills out the picture that is presented to us here. I think that is pretty clear.

Now to come back to our point, as to the substance of the assembly being there when Christ loved it and delivered Himself up for it, I believe it was there in the disciples; the substance was there.

Ques.   When would it be proper to say that the Lord began to love the assembly?

C.A.C. When He received the disciples as the Father's gift: "They were thine, and thou gavest them me", John 17:6. There was something there which could be said to belong to the Father, and it is important for us to recognise that we belonged to the Father before we belonged to Christ. It has helped me a good deal to put Ephesians alongside the gospel of John. In John we see everything is traced by the Lord to the Father, and of His disciples He could say, "They were thine", and He could also say, "They are not of the world, as I am not of the world", John 17:16. That is wonderful and it seems to suggest a very similar thought to "His own flesh".

Ques.   Does that follow on chapter 12, the corn of wheat?

C.A.C.   There, of course, the fruit is looked at as the result of His death, but "They were thine" was before His death.

Rem.   John 12 would be the Son of man type, but this is hardly that; this is the wife of Christ, not the bride.

C.A.C.   Well, quite so, but this runs very much with the gospel of John. Everything in Ephesians is traced to the sovereign purpose of God; it goes back into eternity; the saints were chosen in Christ before the foundation of the world. In John they are the subjects of the Father's work and the Lord receives them as from the Father, and they are not of the world, even as He is not of the world. There was correspondence between Him and them, correspondence so close that you might say they were His own flesh. We see the great capability of the disciples. The Lord says, "If ye were of the world, the world would love its own; but because ye are not of the world, but I have chosen you out of the world, on account of this the world hates you. Remember the word which I said unto you, The bondman is not greater than his master. If they have persecuted me, they will also persecute you … But they will do all these things to you on account of my name, because they have not known him that sent me", John 15:19-21. How perfectly the Lord identifies them with Himself, "If they have kept my word, they will keep also yours". They are viewed as having the same word, so they get the same reception from the world as He got. He says, "I have manifested thy name to the men whom thou gavest me out of the world … and they have kept thy word. Now they have known that all things that thou hast given me are of thee; for the words which thou hast given me I have given them, and they have received them, and have known truly that I came out from thee and have believed that thou sentest me", John 17:6-8. There was a company of persons there before the eye of the Lord who could take account of all the things that the Father had given to the Son, and could trace them to their proper source. They knew that all was of the Father, and whatever words the Father gave Him, He had given them. There was such correspondence spiritually between Him and them that you might say they were morally His own flesh. Substance was there; the spiritual substance of the assembly was there in the disciples and it was there to be loved by Christ. John's gospel brings out very definitely that He loved them. He could say, "As the Father has loved me, I also have loved you", John 15:9. Think of that! That is not Christ loving poor sinners, is it? "As the Father has loved me" - what a love of infinite complacency! There was everything in the Son that was complacent to the Father's love. Now, He says, that is the way I love you. It was a love of complacency because there was spiritual substance there in which He could be complacent. I believe that gives the idea of the love of Christ for the assembly; it is not a sovereign love; it is a complacent love.

Ques.   You refer to the disciples, not to the apostles?

C.A.C.   These things could not be limited to the twelve, because while the twelve are prominently in view, they are in a sense representative of the whole company. What the Lord says of them was not confined to the twelve. That is brought out by the way that section of the gospel begins; it begins by saying, "Having loved his own"; it is not 'having loved the twelve'. There is great force in that "his own" and I should rather connect it spiritually with the thought of His own flesh, that which is of Himself.

Ques.   When you speak of substance,

do you refer to what was actually existing at that time? Is this the result of counsel coming into being?

C.A.C. That is right; the thing has come into being, and I believe the church was there, in substance, to be loved by the Lord in the days of His flesh. The substance was there and it has helped me to understand a statement of Mr. Raven's, which at the time rather puzzled me, and that was, 'We shall never understand the relations between Christ and the assembly unless we understand His relations with His own when He was with them here'. There was a little company, the product of the Father's work, drawn to the Son and having capacity to receive from the Son the words which the Father had given to Him. The Father gives certain words to the Son and the Son in His turn gives these words to His own; there was the same kind of competency in them that there was in Him; I do not say to the same degree, but the same kind of competency. That is what I call substance, and the Lord discerned it there and loved it; it won His affections. I believe that gives us a spiritual view of the love of Christ for the assembly. It is the Father's gift to Him and therefore He could say of that company such marvellous words as, "That they may be one, as we"; that is astonishing! "That they may be one, as we are one". Think of the oneness of the Father and the Son - a oneness that is altogether divine! Now, He says, "That they may be one, as we are one"; what wonderful substance must be there if the saints can be unified with the same kind of oneness as subsists between the Father and the Son! What a marvellous idea it gives of the assembly! That is the divine conception of the assembly: it is His own flesh. I feel how little one has entered into it, our thoughts are so superficial, but the assembly in its actual substance is the worthy object of the affections of Christ.

Ques. Referring to John 13, it says, He "loved them to the end". Would that be in keeping with the thought of Christ delivering Himself up for it?

C.A.C. Yes, right through, and to my mind it goes very much with Ephesians 5. I would commend it to the brethren to study the chapters in John, from the thirteenth to the seventeenth, and ponder over them, and pray over them, alongside what we have in Ephesians 5. There is the thought of a purifying and cleansing service in John 13 and 15, and it is all part of the active service of the love of Christ. Christ purifies the assembly by the washing of water by the word, and John 13 and 15 speak of a cleansing that is brought about by the word. If we think of the nourishing and cherishing I do not know a better scripture to go to for it than those chapters in John. The wonderful nourishing and cherishing of the love of Christ! He seems to give Himself up to it in these chapters. What we have here is the service of His love; that is what the Spirit of God would engage us with and it is well to ponder these chapters in John as showing both the nourishing and the cherishing of the love of Christ.

We perhaps think that in some unknown way Christ will nourish and cherish us, but I believe that the nourishing and cherishing are very specific, and that we have the very substance of it in these chapters in John's gospel. Christ delights to nourish the assembly, to impart to it every element of strength; the idea of nourishing is that elements of growth and strength are made available. Think of the nourishing elements that are in these chapters in the gospel of John, elements that minister to strength and to prosperity and growth! They cannot be surpassed. Chief of all is the knowledge of the Father; how nourishing that is! We can all of us have a good time in praying over these chapters from thirteen to seventeen and regarding them as the unfolding to our hearts of that in which the nourishing and cherishing of Christ for the assembly consists; the substance of it is there.

"In order that he might sanctify it", that is, that it may correspond with Himself, because in John's gospel He is the sanctified One. He is marked out distinctly as the Father's sanctified One and He is the One who sanctifies Himself. Now the saints are to be all of one with Him in that; they are to be His own flesh in that particular.

Ques.   Is this in view in Acts 19, where the apostle separates the Ephesians?

C.A.C.   We see there a company of persons set apart from all the influences of this world, even its religious influences, because he separated them from the synagogue, not merely from the worship of Diana, and no doubt as separated they came under nourishing and cherishing influences. The knowledge of the Father is one of the most nourishing things that you can think of. The Lord says, "Henceforth ye know him and have seen him" (John 14:7); what nourishment for the soul, what stability! And then He speaks of the Comforter, how nourishing that is! A divine Person coming to be with them - in them. And then there is the thought of being able to draw every supply from Christ Himself. He says, "Abide in me", how nourishing that is! These are the great divine realities by which the assembly is nourished. I am just suggesting the thought, that every one may follow up individually the great nourishing and strengthening principles that are brought out in these chapters.

And then there is the cherishing; cherishing stimulates affection. A man might give his wife plenty to eat, but if he did not cherish her, her affections would wane. Now the Lord not only nourishes the assembly viewed as His own flesh, but He cherishes it, and so we get all those lovely touches of affection in these chapters in John. They are very beautiful. Just take all that the Lord says about His own love for His own, and the Father's love, and the mutual love of the saints among themselves, and you have something of the reality of Christ cherishing His own flesh. He gives the warmth and comfort of divine love; it is all very beautiful.

Ques.   Is what you have been speaking of what the apostle refers to as "This mystery is great"?

C.A.C.   Yes. Paul says, so to speak, I began to talk about wives and husbands but my mind was really full of Christ and the assembly. He uses the affectionate relations of husband and wife as the frame-work and he fits into that the whole precious truth of

Christ and the assembly. It is very lovely.

Ques.   Thus we are taken right away from the material thing; is not that what should happen at a marriage meeting?

C.A.C.   Before the end of a really good marriage meeting Christ and the assembly would be in view rather than the bride and bridegroom, and to their own hearts also.

Ques.   Would the presentation of that Person bring the substance to light?

C.A.C.   Christ is like a great magnet let down into this world. If you put a powerful magnet into a lot of rubbish of all sorts, you would find that every particle of iron and steel, everything that was kindred, would be attracted to it. Pieces of brass and wood would not be attracted, but iron and steel being kindred with the magnet would be drawn to it. Now Christ came in as the great magnet and everything that was kindred with Him was attracted to Him. There was substance there, that which was in substance His own flesh, and He loved it and devoted Himself in love to it.

Ques.   Would you say that with regard to the disciples it was only after His resurrection and ascension?

C.A.C.   Undoubtedly the substance was there before. All these wonderful statements in John's gospel were true before; they were true of the disciples.

Rem.   The assembly proper does not come to light until after.

C.A.C.   Of course it did not come to light formally, but the substance of which it is comprised did. The substance of it was there, that is the point. In the disciples there was substance that corresponded with Christ, so that He could discern what was there in correspondence with Himself, His counterpart.

Rem.   It was the work of the Father.

C.A.C.   It was the product of the Father's work, and therefore it surpasses any type. A certain type presents a certain feature; you have to keep to that feature. If you try to make it say something it was not intended to say, you do it violence. Different types bring out certain features, but when you come to the reality in Christ and the assembly, there is a fulness and detail and perfections that you cannot get in any of the types; it includes the types and goes beyond them. The Lord Himself surpasses every type of Him. The great object of the writer of the epistle to the Hebrews was to show that He surpassed everything. He surpassed Moses and Aaron and Joshua, all of them, even Melchisedec. The types and the promises were like stars shining in the darkness of the midnight sky, but when the sun rises it is seen to surpass them all; you feel now we have what surpasses them all.

Ques. Does Luke 10 approach what you have been saying?

C.A.C. Yes, I think so. There are scriptures in the Old Testament which give intimations, suggestions. The prophets and the righteous men had exercises and desires but they never really saw the substance. Now the Lord can say, "Blessed are the eyes which see the things that ye see", Luke 10:23. They saw the substance of everything in Christ and Christ was in them by the Father's work in them, so that there was substance on both sides. The Lord would clothe these precious scriptures in John's gospel with power for the nourishing and cherishing of our souls, so that we may be strong in all the features that mark the assembly as the wife of Christ, having ardent affections, produced and called into activity under the cherishing of Christ. The important thing that Paul had before him was that we should understand that the assembly is one flesh with Christ. He says, "This mystery is great, but I speak as to Christ, and as to the assembly". It is definitely a mystery and we have to be initiated into it, otherwise we do not know anything about it. We should pray for initiation; we need it. One of the most nourishing things that the Lord brings before His disciples in these chapters in John is the suggestion of their liberty to pray. Nothing is more remarkable than the positive character of the Lord's words as to prayer. They are very strengthening because there is no limit, absolutely no limit, to what we can get from the Father and the Son. He says, "And whatsoever ye shall ask in my name, this will I do, that the Father may be glorified in the Son", John 14:13. We do not really believe it, I am afraid, but there it is, that is part of His nourishing. As those who are His own flesh, we should not want a single thing that was not for His name; we should not have a personal or selfish thought in our mind; our asking would be for His name. That is suitable to His wife; she has lost her own name and bears His. That is the proper idea of a wife; He called their name Adam.

In these chapters in John we see a company of persons who have lost their own interests, their own name, and they ask in His name; now that is the substance of the wife. Asking in His name is for His interests, His honour, His glory, for the promotion of what is before Him. Then there is the absolute certainty of the answer; He says, I will do it; and He says, as to the Father, "I say not to you that I will demand of the Father for you, for the Father himself has affection for you", John 16:26, 27. It is as much as to say, He will be delighted to do it. How nourishing it is!

The interests of the wife are merged in those of her husband. She might have had fifty interests of her own before, but when married all her interests are merged in her husband's interests, and so the heart of her husband doth safely trust in her.

Ques.   Does the wife become the bride?

C.A.C.   Yes, I think so. John speaks of the bride; Paul speaks of the espoused virgin and the wife. The gospels speak of the bride, but we never see her in the gospels. We find the bridegroom and the sons of the bridechamber and the virgins that go to meet the bridegroom. We get all the accompaniments of the scene without the bride actually coming into view. The bride is never seen until she comes out with Christ, but she is heard before she is seen, for there is the possibility of hearing the voice of the bride. It is heard in that marvellous one word which concentrates in itself the whole affection of the bride - "The Spirit and the bride say, Come", Revelation 22:17.

Rem.   She is not complete yet.

C.A.C.   Nevertheless there is a bridal

character of things. John the baptist says, "He that has the bride is the bridegroom". The bride then was formed of those who were leaving John and going to Jesus; the bride was there in John's estimation, and he was glad that the Bridegroom should have her. The bride is there all the time, viewed characteristically. Of course, in the complete sense, the thought of the bride will not be filled out until the whole of the church company is translated, but she is there all the time, essentially and characteristically.

Rem.   We used to sing, 'For Thee Thy bride has tarried long', but you would hardly sing that now.

C.A.C.   I think it is right in principle. The vitality and life of the bride, the affections suitable to her, should always be there. The result of Jesus' testimony being rendered in the assemblies is that "the Spirit and the bride say, Come". Whatever has bridal character in the assemblies says 'Come', so that I think the bride may be viewed as always present though, of course, not yet in display. But her affections can be appealed to: "I Jesus have sent mine angel to testify these things to you in the assemblies", Revelation 22:16. He presents Himself as "the bright and morning star. And the Spirit and the bride say, Come". It is a characteristic

Reading at Exeter

18 January 1933

Ephesians 6:1-9

C.A.C. It is very striking how many precious thoughts are brought together in the Christian household; it would seem to suggest to us that God intended every Christian household to be a treasury of divine thoughts, so that we get in the husband and wife the thought of the headship of Christ and the place of the assembly as standing in relation to Christ as Head. Then we get the family idea, which is another most important part of the counsel of God. Then, finally, we get the thought of service, and that brings in another universal thought of God. I believe to get the scope of this scripture would bring us in view of all the great thoughts which God purposes to work out in His saints, and they are all enshrined in the Christian household.

Ques. Is this confined to the Christian household in this epistle? What about children who have unconverted parents?

C.A.C. Well, you see, principles that are established in the Christian household would hold good universally, so it would appear that God establishes certain principles in a Christian household which have universal scope, in keeping with the character of the epistle. The greatest principle in the moral universe is the headship of Christ, and it is set forth in every Christian husband. These immense things are brought down and exemplified in that way, and so the wife represents the great principle of subjection to headship, not lordship, but subjection to headship, and I suppose that is an eternal principle. I think lordship will not be needed in eternity because everything will be in new creation setting, and it will be a matter of subjection to headship. Now that eternal principle is embodied in the assembly and illustrated in every Christian wife. God's primary thought was headship, and the assembly is brought in as the subject vessel getting the gain of headship in subjection. The second great thought of God is the family thought, and I suppose the family thought is going to be established fully in the universe. It is brought out in this very epistle that God's thought is to have many families; that is, the family idea is an essential part of the counsel of God, and it is illustrated in every Christian family, so that the saints are addressed in this epistle as of the household of God - that is, they are in the children's place; they are of the household; and the saints are exhorted to be imitators of God as beloved children. That is the family thought and presently God is going to fill a universe with many families, heavenly families and earthly families, for there will be earthly families throughout eternity as well as heavenly. The family thought of God is going to be universal, and yet God has embodied it in every Christian household; it is very interesting and profoundly instructive. Further, the principle of service is a universal principle of God and will be so eternally, everything being absolutely at God's disposal and at the disposal of Christ. Now you see that particular part of the counsel of God is set forth in servants, but it is a universal principle - we all come in, every saint is a slave. So the three different relations are covered by the relations in which the saints stand. We stand as wife in relation to Christ as Head; we stand as children in relation to God as Father, the family thought, and we stand as slaves in relation to Christ as Lord; so the principles illustrated in the Christian household are universal. It becomes the privilege of the husband to exemplify the great principle of headship and the privilege of the wife to exemplify the great principle of subjection in relation to headship; it becomes the privilege of the children in a Christian household to exemplify the universal principle that governs the family of God, and it becomes the privilege of slaves to exemplify the relations to Christ as Lord which are proper to all saints. It enlarges and magnifies the position.

Ques.   Would you say a little more as to headship?

C.A.C.   Headship is a question of influence rather than authority, and that is very important as having its source in God Himself. I suppose the greatest truth in Scripture - if we may venture to single out one truth and speak of it in that way - is the truth of the headship of God: "The Christ's head God", 1 Corinthians 11:3. David was in the light of the headship of God; he says, "Thou art exalted as Head above all; and riches and glory are of thee", 1 Chronicles 29:11, 12. He is in the presence of the headship of God. Now we see in Christ One who ever looked up with reverence and affection to God as His Head. He was always influenced by God, no other influence ever controlled Him; so every Christian man is to look up to Christ as his Head, to be influenced by Christ, and if we look up to Him with reverence and affection we shall be influenced by Him. This principle comes down from God to Christ, and from Christ to the Christian man, and from the Christian man to his wife, so that a holy and divine influence is extended in that way. Influence is not exactly like law. For instance, the king of this country is the king and he has authority. If he gives an order it has to be obeyed - that is authority. But the king is also the head of society in this country, and the way the king behaves influences the whole of the society of the country. If the king is a moral man and a religious man, his influence would pervade every part of society; if he is a licentious man, that influence would pervade society. Now it seems to me that these are the thoughts connected with headship - influence that controls, not exactly by authority, but by the character of the person to whom we look up as head.

Ques.   Is that why you said that lordship does not go through while headship does?

C.A.C.   It seems to me that the idea of God being all in all is the thought of headship, the eternal headship of God.

Ques.   Does lordship generally suggest authority in adverse elements?

C.A.C.   I thought so, and I think lordship comes out in connection with the slave. The principle of lordship is illustrated and exemplified in the conduct of Christian slaves. They are regarded, in a sense, as forming part of the household. The husband, wife, children and slaves. You have to put them all together to get the divine thought. We are all part of the wife, and every Christian man has to take up the thought of headship; and we are all children, and we are all slaves. God has been pleased to bring these great universal principles together and to put them into the Christian household as a treasury.

Ques.   I think I can see the wife side and the family side going through, but I am not quite clear about the service side. Is that an eternal thought, too?

C.A.C.   It is certainly a universal thought at the present time.

Rem.   I had thought, giving it a more direct application to children, that it is a wonderful favour that it is addressed to children here.

C.A.C.   That is the beauty of it, that every child has such an important place as being privileged to take up in such a way a principle that belongs to the whole family of God, that every Christian child is privileged to carry that part of the counsel of God in practical experience by obedience and by honouring his parents. It is the working out in one little child of God's family idea, so that the widest scope of things is exemplified in the behaviour of one little child. I think it is very beautiful.

Rem. So that we see working in the Christian household the principle that will put everything right eventually for the pleasure of God.

C.A.C. Yes, and every child in the Christian household has to acknowledge that the Lord has put him in that place and in that relationship, so that he is to obey his parents in the Lord; the Lord has put him there.

Ques. It goes much beyond the law, does it not? The law never addressed children in this way.

C.A.C. It told them they were to honour their father and mother, which is a little more than obeying them. To honour one's parents is to regard them highly, so that they are held in esteem, not merely obeyed. A child might obey a policeman who told him to cross the road, or not, but Christian parents are to be the subject of honour. That is what God looks for in His children, that He should be honoured. He says, "If then I be a father, where is mine honour?" Malachi 1:6. God looks for honour from His children and that they should look up to Him as the model; they have God before them as a model. That is what I understand by honouring one's father and mother: they are honoured by being looked up to as models, and that is what is meant in this same epistle - "Be ... imitators of God, as beloved children", Ephesians 5:1. I believe the thought of imitation is bound up in the thought of honouring parents; you honour them by giving them the place of models. The right family idea is that the father is the model. The Lord brought that out very fully in what people call the sermon on the mount, that if God is known as Father He becomes the model, and that the children are to be formed by the character of the Father. It is the outcome of owning the place that we have as children in the affections of the Father; that is, what leads a child properly to obey and to honour his parents is the sense of the place of affection.

Ques.   In a very wide dispensational aspect, would you link these four with Christ, the assembly, Israel and the nations?

C.A.C.   I do not think that you could quite tie them down in that way, because the family thought could not be limited to Israel and the thought of service could not be limited to the nations. They will all come into these thoughts. The thought of headship and of the wife belongs to Israel as well as to the assembly, and the family idea will be there, too, because in the very place where they have been known as rejected they will be known as the sons of the living God.

Rem.　It seems very wonderful that God has designed to have in the assembly the working out of things that will be universal presently.

C.A.C.　Yes, and it is very wonderful that God should put all these thoughts into one house. It gives you a great idea of the Christian household and enables you to understand how the assembly is related to households. I think it is very beautiful because it is the divine thought, and children will find it to their advantage; it says so. It is rather remarkable that there is this one feature of earthly blessing brought over into Christianity because Christianity is a system of spiritual and heavenly blessing. So if children want to live long they had better mind how they behave.

The divine idea is that children in the household are in the presence of headship in the father and in the presence of subjection to headship in their mother, so that there are features there which command honour. There is that which a right-minded child respects. There is such a thing as parents having the respect of their children. I think I could say that I respected my parents. I respected them for the spiritual qualities that I was able to discern in them even as a little child. Now that is what I think is meant by the word "honour", and that kind of honour never ceases. If there are spiritual qualities in the parents the child never ceases to honour them, however old he gets, and the older he gets the more he honours the memory of the spiritual features that influenced him when he was a little child. And so the parent, the father, is not to provoke the children to anger, but to bring them up (that is the very same word as is translated 'nourish' in the previous chapter, where it speaks of the Lord nourishing and cherishing the assembly) in the discipline and admonition of the Lord. That is, the Christian father has himself been under the discipline and admonition of the Lord and he nourishes his children in that which he himself has learned to be very beneficial. He brings it to bear on the children as one that has learned how beneficial it is, so that he nourishes his children, he makes that food for them. It is not the rod, but a nourishing influence, and I believe that a Christian father who has himself been under the discipline and admonition of the Lord and has proved how good and valuable it is has acquired wealth, and the wealth that he has acquired he passes on to his children. We are all familiar with the thought of a parent amassing money to leave to his children, but the Christian parent is not concerned about that so much, he is concerned about being a model for his children, so that there is nothing better that they could do than to imitate him. What he has acquired and found so beneficial for himself under the discipline and admonition of the Lord he passes on to them, so that they inherit his spiritual substance. Now that is far more important than that he should leave them ten thousand pounds! The thing to see is that the child grows up just like his father, so that everybody would say, 'How like his father that boy is'.

And so Paul says of Timothy, "As a child a father, he has served with me in the work of the glad tidings", Philippians 2:22. That is what he means when he says to the Corinthians, 'I am going to send Timothy and when he comes he will put you in mind of my ways as they are in Christ'. Now I do not think that Timothy was going to remind them by word of mouth but the very way he would carry on amongst them would make them say, 'He is exactly like Paul. Paul's ways are in Christ, Timothy's ways are in Christ, is he not like Paul?' The divine idea as to children is that they are to imitate their parents. That raises much exercise for parents; if I have a family would it be the very best thing in view of time and eternity if my children imitated me in every detail? Could I honestly say that would be the very best thing for them for time and eternity? That is the position. Now, you see, that would lead to the children not only obeying but honouring, and if a child honours his father he will imitate him, and he will do things in the same kind of way and in the same spirit that his father does them. That is the proper family idea. God is going to have many families and is going to put the impress of Christ on every one of those families so that they will all be like Him; they will all correspond with God as the universal Father.

Rem.　　In Colossians obedience is enjoined in all things.

C.A.C.　　I suppose obedience is the most essential principle possible. Whatever relationship there is, obedience has some part in it.

Ques.　　Would the principle of the promise that they would live long on the earth apply to all as the children of God?

C.A.C.　　Yes, and I think God brings it in as a particular encouragement to children as moving in obedience and in honouring their parents. He brings in this remarkable touch in Ephesians, that you have a promise of living long on the earth. We all ought to have before us that it is a desirable thing that our ways should be such that it will be consistent with God's plan to keep us here a long time, and it is a privilege to be here as those who are imitating God as His children.

Ques.   Have you in mind that it takes in the thought of health?

C.A.C. Yes, these principles are very advantageous; it says, "that it may be well with thee". It will be well, and I have observed in the course of my life that it is well for children to obey and honour their parents; it does work out very well.

Ques.   Is there anything in the nature of an arbitrary command in the absence of characteristics which are worthy of honour?

C.A.C. Well, I think we have to take it altogether. Of course, if a believing child has parents that are not, as we should say, worthy of honour personally, the relationship is. However morally defective persons may be, the relationship is to be honoured.

Then, as to service - slaves. Every Christian slave was in that position in order to display his relation to Christ and to the will of God, and to the Lord. His position brought out that there was something about him infinitely greater than his place as a slave.

He was one who stood in a most wonderful relation to Christ as Lord and to the will of God, and the low position in which he was found socially was a proper setting for his relations to Christ as Lord and for the will of God to come out. And, you see, we are all slaves; we are all children and we are all slaves. I would not like to suggest the re-establishment of slavery as an institution amongst men, but I feel pretty sure that we have lost something as to our moral apprehension of things by its abolition. I think we have lost the sense of being the absolute property of another.

A servant now, if he is uncomfortable and does not like his place, leaves. Now that idea could never enter the mind of a slave, he was the absolute property of his master, and he had to do everything that his master said. The apostle clothes that position with glory; he shows that that very position is going to bring out your relations to Christ as Lord and to the will of God.

Rem.   So the slave here is the absolute property, in a sense, of two masters.

C.A.C.   The slave finds that his relations with his earthly master are to be the occasions of bringing out his relations to his heavenly Master. And so it is in any subordinate position that any of us may fill. Whatever position it is, it is just the framework into which the beautiful picture is put of our relations to Christ as Lord. Now I wonder if we have looked at our work in that light, whether it is behind the counter or in the workshop, or whatever it is? That is the framework of the picture, but then what is to be in the frame are the relations in which we stand to Christ as Lord. Now that glorifies what we may call the inferior relations in which many of us are placed.

Ques.　Do we see that in the little captive maid?

C.A.C.　What a beautiful example is there! What dignity! She is a slave, but look at the dignity! She is thinking about Israel's God. She is governed in her menial duties, and as to her affections by the thought of the wonderful God whom she served. She had served Him in Israel, and now she has been taken captive and she is serving Him still. She wears all the dignity of a servant of Jehovah in the house of a heathen general. It is very fine! She thinks of his good, she is far superior to Naaman; outwardly in a very inferior position she is morally superior to everybody in the house.

Rem.　She was exactly doing what slaves are exhorted to do here, "Doing the will of God", and so on.

C.A.C. The words used here are very beautiful: "In simplicity of your heart as to the Christ", and "As bondmen of Christ, doing the will of God from the soul". It is very fine. Now these things are as important for us, for we are all slaves. We all come in as children, but then we all come in as slaves, and what is very remarkable here is that the masters are slaves, too. So that there is what you might call a very inconsistent exhortation! I do not know whether we have all noticed it, but it says to the masters, "Masters, do the same things towards them". We should not have expected that, should we? Do the same things - that is, the masters are just to be characterised by the very same things that characterise the servants, simplicity of heart and subjection to the Lord and, he says, Remember you have a Master up in heaven and He is no respecter of persons. That is, the very same exhortations that are addressed to the slaves are just the right things for the master, too.

Ques. What do you mean when you say we are all slaves?

C.A.C. That we are all in that relation to Christ; we are absolutely in that relation, and I believe we have greatly lost the sense of it. We hardly know anything about slavery now; it has almost disappeared from the world, but the idea of slaves is in each one of the epistles; each one of the five apostles who have written epistles writes to us as slaves of Jesus Christ. Each of them speaks of himself as a slave, and we are all in that relation to Christ, not at liberty for our own wills but bondslaves or bondmen of the Lord. We think sometimes that we can do a little bit for the Lord when we think fit; well, that is the voluntary principle, but I have to recognise that I am not a volunteer; I am committed to it, body, soul and spirit, as a slave, and I can never be anything else day or night but a slave of Jesus Christ - His absolutely.

I believe we need to consider more the thought of recompense. Paul brings that in, he says, "Whatever good each shall do, this he shall receive of the Lord". The Lord would have the thought of recompense very much before us; He brought it very much before His disciples. If you are a slave, and are committed, the absolute property of Christ, and you serve Him every minute, so to speak, of the twenty-four hours of the day, you will be recompensed; every bit that is good will be recompensed. I think if we kept that before us it would make us more diligent in service.

———————

Reading at Exeter

25 January 1933

Ephesians 6:10-24

C.A.C.   There is great blessedness unfolded to us in this epistle. Paul opened out to us all that was in his heart; he has made known what has been given to him by the grace of God, the knowledge of the mystery and the unsearchable riches of the Christ. He has announced the full counsel of God. We could hardly expect anything else than that it would be the subject of attack on the part of the power of evil; it would be strange if it were not so. The present work of God is more wonderful than it has been at any previous period, more wonderful, in a sense, than it ever will be again. The full height of divine thought has been brought out, and brought out not only under the view of the saints, but under the view of principalities and powers in the heavenlies. Some of them will learn in it the all-various wisdom of God, and some of them are roused to intense hostility; so that if the assembly becomes the lesson-book for angels, as it has been said, on the other hand it becomes the target of deadly hatred and opposition on the part of wicked spirits.

W.W.   Do we regard the opposition here as having in view to prevent the saints entering into the import of what has been brought out in this epistle?

C.A.C.   It would work that way undoubtedly. The saints are viewed as occupying the position from which the enemies have been dislodged, so that the issue is that when the battles are over you stand still on the field; you occupy the ground. Having done all, having overcome all things, you stand. After every foe has been put forth the saints are still standing; they hold the position; they hold the heavenly ground.

But I had thought that this chapter is rather the converse of what happened in the history of Elisha. There was a time when Elisha prayed for his servant and he said, "Jehovah, I pray thee, open his eyes that he may see" (2 Kings 6:17), and when the young man's eyes were opened he saw the whole mountain filled with horses and chariots of fire round Elisha. He was allowed to have a glimpse of the invisible powers that were acting in consort with the prophet at that time. Now this seems to be the converse of that. That is, Paul would open our eyes to see the tremendous character of the evil powers. We are often like the young man, not having our eyes opened to the true character of the invisible powers. These in Ephesians 6 are invisible powers arraigned against what is of God, and it is well for us to have our eyes opened to this. We shall not realise the nature of the conflict or the necessity for the armour if we do not realise the tremendous forces that are against us, because this is not human opposition or persecution. That is not contemplated here at all. It says our conflict is not with blood and flesh; it is not what man can do, but a power far greater than that of men operating, and operating with great skill. Men are often stupid and foolish in their opposition to God, but the spiritual powers in the heavenlies are never stupid; they are never foolish. There is a sagacity and subtlety that can only be defeated by divine power.

F.J.T.   I have a little difficulty as to these powers. It says, "Having ascended up on high, he has led captivity captive", Ephesians 4:8. How would you reconcile the two?

C.A.C.   I thought there was a sense, a very blessed and full sense, in which it could be said that Christ has spoiled principalities and powers.

F.J.T.   Would that apply to these powers?

C.A.C.   Yes, I thought so. In the cross the whole power of evil is really broken, but that is only known to faith, because the power is not actually broken publicly yet. Is not that just the position? All around us in the world we see the powers of evil going on unchecked, the lawlessness of men, and every kind of opposition to God. But for faith every evil power has been vanquished in the cross of our Lord Jesus Christ. He has overcome every foe, but the results of the victory are not yet manifested. So I believe all these wicked spirits know that their doom is sealed, like the one who is their ruler, Satan. It says in Revelation 12 that when the serpent is cast out of heaven he comes down to the earth having great rage, knowing that he has but a short time. That is, he knows he is a defeated foe. But, you see, knowing that he is a defeated foe does not in the slightest degree diminish his hostility or his malice, or hinder him from using every form of subtlety against Christ or against what is of God. So that having had their death-blow, they have been spoiled and Christ is now dividing the spoil with His saints. He has given gifts to men and every gift is the proof of His victory; yet publicly the enemy is still at large, and active in a terrible way. Hence this spiritual conflict has to be taken up and we have to "be strong in the Lord, and in the might of his strength" and to put on the armour - there is nothing else for it.

And there is overcoming power in the saints; that is what has come out in the saints in all ages. God had intimated through the prophet Daniel that there would be certain saints who would be saints of the high places, saints with heavenly places, and we find that the beast and the antichrist are against them and seek to wear them out. It says, "He ... shall wear out the saints of the most high places" (Daniel 7:25), but then we find that in spite of all his efforts to wear them out, their people get the kingdom; they are proved overcomers.

W.W.   Would that be involved in the apostle saying he had kept the faith?

C.A.C.   I think that is the language of a man who had to face all these powers and had overcome them and is found standing at the end on the ground that is of God; he has not surrendered a hair's breadth.

F.B.   Would there be a reason for these powers being distinguished?

C.A.C.   I think he used these titles of dignity with a reason, principalities, authorities, universal lords of this darkness, spiritual power of wickedness in the heavenlies. It gives us the idea of the extraordinary character of the powers. He applied titles of great eminence and dignity to them, showing that these are not ordinary demons, such as might take possession of a poor human being and seek in every way to degrade and destroy him. These powers are far above that; these are fallen angels, and they act really as princes in the kingdom of darkness. We need to have a sense of what one might call the exalted character of the powers of evil. Satan himself is spoken of as a dignitary; we are apt to forget that. I think it is necessary for us to understand that we have to do with evil powers that are by no means contemptible; they are not powers that you can think lightly of. I believe there is nothing more lacking amongst Christians than a proper sense of the greatness and dignity of the powers of evil. If that is understood we realise that no human power or sagacity could possibly stand against them; nothing but the Lord and the might of His strength will do that. So that if we are not strong in the Lord and in the might of His strength we shall be driven from the field.

F.B.   How are these powers wielded against us?

C.A.C.   Well, they are wielded on the line of strategy - it says "the artifices of the devil". That is, it is not violent power like persecution, but it is the artifices, it is subtlety. It says that the serpent was more subtle than any beast of the field, and we find that Satan transforms himself into an angel of light. This kind of thing is seen in people who come and prove every single thing they say from the Scriptures, and yet their object is deadly hostility against what is of God. They handle the Scriptures with consummate skill to prove that the lie is the truth. It is not done foolishly; we must not expect to find things done foolishly; they are done with a subtlety that is far above the power of man. That is what we have to face. This kind of opposition would come out through teachings; the vessels would be men, but the apostle is not thinking here of the vessels. The vessels would be like those of whom he speaks in 2 Corinthians 11, false apostles, deceitful workers and, he says, they are ministers of Satan, transforming themselves as ministers of righteousness. There is a great pretence of only wanting what is right and what is according to Scripture. I had a letter from a man last week, a great pretension of only wanting what is right and what is according to Scripture, but his object was to deny the most fundamental and most precious truths in Scripture. That is, transformed as a minister of righteousness and that is where you get artifices. A man gets up and gives a nice word; every word of it is founded on Scripture but Satan's object in it is to oppose and resist something that the Spirit of God may be calling attention to at the time. Now that is where the artifices of the devil work.

Ques.　How can we detect it?

C.A.C.　We detect it by occupying the ground that is attacked. Those who occupy the ground are able to detect what is contrary to it. It is those who have the benefit of the epistle who are addressed. He says, 'I have opened out to you the whole counsel of God; now you are going to be mercilessly attacked. This is all so precious; it is so infinitely exalted that the most tremendous forces of evil are going to come into action to move you away from it and nothing will keep you but to be strong in the Lord and in the might of His strength, and then you must actually put on the whole armour of God. You must get the might of the Lord's strength, you must be girded with it, invested with it, by putting on the armour. It is as we put on the armour that we get the might of the Lord's strength really with us, so that it is not only that the power is there in Him, but we are so strong in it that it is here with us. The armour is really the power of the Lord with His people, and they are invested with the might of the strength of the One who is at God's right hand, and the enemy can do nothing.

Ques. Would you say that the object of every attack is the Person of Christ?

C.A.C. I am sure that is right, because all that is of God is in Christ. Whether it is the declaration of God or the establishment of His thoughts, it is all in Christ. And then, of course, the assembly as being the closest to Him and really identified with Him, is opposed, but it is because of its identification with Christ.

F.J.T. Is it true today that the joy of the Lord is our strength?

C.A.C. I think that is so. The writer has been telling us plenty to make us so, has he not? He has been telling us all about the unsearchable riches of Christ, and now having furnished us and enriched us he says, 'Now, look out! There is going to be a tremendous attack'.

F.J.T. It does not say, 'Be strong in Christ Jesus', but "in the Lord".

C.A.C. Yes, he brings in the title of dignity which is suitable, because he is going to speak of the lords of this darkness. The Lord is superior to all the power of evil; there is no question about that. So that while the present time is a time of greatest possible blessing, yet from another point of view it is the evil day, and we have to take account of that.

F.J.T. Would you help us as to putting on the armour of God?

C.A.C. It seems to me to suggest that the different parts of the armour are only acquired through personal exercises, because we have to be personally invested with these things. These are not abstract truths; it is not truth and righteousness and salvation as abstractly known, or even as things you might know in Christ. That is not the point here, but it is that they are personally identified with us, so that there is an exercise, a distinct exercise, connected with each part of the armour. Therefore the saints become characterised by certain things, that is, the breastplate of righteousness is something connected with what I am. It does not say righteousness in Christ, but righteousness is to mark me in all my ways and behaviour and character, so that I have no fear in meeting the enemy. My breast is not exposed, everything is right.

Rem. These things are spoken of in Isaiah in the way in which God Himself seems to have put them on.

C.A.C. Yes, it is very striking in Isaiah 59 that Jehovah comes out as invested with these things. When Jehovah deals with the powers of evil, He comes out as invested with similar features. It has often been said that Ephesians 6 is the appearing of Christ anticipated. The second chapter anticipates the rapture; that is, the saints are raised and seated in the heavenlies and that is the anticipation of the rapture. In chapter 6 they come out to meet and overcome all the hostile powers of evil, just as the Lord will come out. He will come out to overcome the beast and the antichrist and all the powers of evil presently, and in the meantime the saints are in the evil day and as invested with this armour they overcome.

God has introduced the full splendour of His own wondrous and heavenly thoughts. Now they are to be held, and they are to be held by the same power that will publicly dispossess the power of evil when the Lord comes out of heaven.

Rem.   I suppose it is only as we keep on this ground that we realise wc have opposing forces against us.

C.A.C.   I think so. I think this conflict belongs to those who have known what it is to occupy heavenly ground.

F.J.T.   Is not the armour more defensive than for aggression?

C.A.C.   Well, I suppose it is. The sword is an offensive weapon. The idea is that you hold the ground; it is not exactly making attacks on the enemy, but the enemy is making attacks on you and you overcome him, so that when the battle is over you stand still on the ground; you have not been driven from the field. The position is looked at here as secure; it is the whole counsel of God. It is secure for the saints and they are secure for it. Now the enemy comes up with all his forces; what kind of persons have we to be? We have to be soldiers in the Lord's host, and what kind of armour do we need in order to stand? We all need the armour, so that we are to stand as those who have girded their loins about with truth; that is the first thing.

J.T.B. Would this find prominence in Timothy?

C.A.C. Yes. Paul goes off the scene as an old warrior, and he encourages Timothy to be a good soldier. Now we are all soldiers in Ephesians 6; we are not merely saints or sons but soldiers. It is quite a different figure.

J.B.T. So that it has a special application today in view of 2 Timothy.

C.A.C. Yes, I should think it has. I should think the qualities of soldiers are very necessary today. First of all, we are so girded by truth that it becomes a support to us. I think the point is that truth is consciously a support to us.

F.J.T.   Why the loins?

C.A.C.   I suppose the girding of the loins is always in Scripture a preparation for something strenuous. All through Scripture that is the thought. Jehovah said to Job, "Gird up now thy loins like a man"; it implies something strenuous. Elisha girded up his loins and ran before Ahab a long distance - it was a strenuous action.

Ques.   Why is it the gospel of peace?

C.A.C.   I suppose that is important as characterising the walk of the saints; there should be nothing about their walk but what would prepare the way for the glad tidings of peace. People should be favourably impressed towards the gospel by the walk of the saints, which is to have that peaceful character that would commend the glad tidings of peace.

Ques.   Would you suggest that the conflict is carried to the sphere of the work of God among men?

C.A.C.   I should say that it is the way that the powers of evil are defeated, and they are defeated by very practical features in the saints. These are not theoretical things; they are very practical. To be girded with truth and to have the breastplate of righteousness and the preparation of the glad tidings of peace, and so on, are very practical matters. A good practical state is what qualifies us to stand against the powers of evil.

F.H.B. Is the thought that this conflict is carried on on the part of the saints as standing together in unity? Not just units but the whole company divinely set together and moving as one?

C.A.C. Yes, and all having these characteristics. They are marked by truth and righteousness and peace and faith, wonderful qualities and identified with us personally, so that this is not only what we hold but what holds us.

F.H.B. Would what we get in chapter 4 apply here - "The measure of the stature of the fulness of the Christ"? Would something of that character be required if we are to take any useful part in this conflict?

C.A.C. Yes, I thought it followed on the whole teaching of the epistle. Paul supposes you have all that; now you are to be ready for the opposition. What he has set you in is so precious and so exalted and divine and spiritual in its character that it is going to be assaulted. Now you will have to have certain qualities and characteristics to be able to stand.

F.H.B. In relation to the conflict described

in the book of Joshua, are not these chapters on the line of this?

C.A.C. Well, there is a good deal that corresponds, it seems to me. The one essential difference there is that they were fighting to get possession, but here the fighting is to hold the position. The types do not fit on every point.

F.H.B. I wondered whether chapters 9 and 10 were more like this than chapters 6 and 8.

C.A.C. I think that is right.

A.T. What do you think of the instance of David's mighty man standing in the midst of the field of barley to deliver it?

C.A.C. That is more the idea; there was something there of God and he held it against the powers of the enemy. That is the idea of this chapter; it is holding things, not fighting to get them, but having been set in them, holding them.

F.B. In 2 Timothy 2:22 it speaks of pursuing righteousness, faith, love, peace. What is the difference between that and this?

C.A.C. Persons are to be marked by the possession of these characteristics. The apostle John could speak of the brethren bearing witness to Gaius - he says they "bore testimony to thy holding fast the truth", 3 John 3. How wonderful that there was a man so characterised by truth that the brethren could talk about it. And then John speaks of him walking in truth (verse 3), not in the truth, but walking in truth. Walking in the truth would be that we walk in the light of what is made known to us. The truth is all that is made known, and as Christians we are to walk in the light of it, but walking in truth is another matter. It is that the walk of the saints is characterised by truth and so all the energies are controlled by truth, the girdle of truth. If any of us is unrighteous in our ways, well, we have no breastplate; if we are not straight in business and other matters, what an advantage it is to the enemy!

F.J.T.   You would give this an entirely present application, not a future one?

C.A.C.   Yes.

———

Reading at Dawlish

6 May 1938

Ephesians 1:13,14; Ephesians 2:18-22;
Ephesians 3:3-6; Ephesians 3:16-19;
Ephesians 4:1-4

L.M.   When we take up Ephesians we find we are introduced into what is spiritual; our blessings at the present time are spiritual blessings. At the end of the book we arrive at spiritual songs, so if we can take it in we are at once introduced into a realm that is spiritual. In the verse we began with (chapter 1: 13) we come in by the sealing of the Spirit; in chapter 2 we have the habitation of God by the Spirit; in chapter 3 we get the mystery which can only be known in the power of the Spirit of God - it was made known to the apostles and prophets by the Spirit; and in chapter 4 we get one Spirit, so there is a line of thought which runs through the epistle. Do you go with that, Mr. Coates?

C.A.C.   Yes, that is confirmed by the thought that the words you read in chapter 1 are part of an utterance of worship. It is very interesting to see that from verse 3 to 14 of chapter 1 it is one sentence; you cannot put a full stop into it, and all is linked on with a note of worship: "Blessed be the God and Father of our Lord Jesus Christ ...". It is a kind of sample of the worship of the assembly. The sealing of the Spirit is to be connected with the God and Father of our Lord Jesus Christ; it gives it a heavenly character.

Ques.   Is the sealing of the Spirit here an advance on Corinthians?

C.A.C.   I thought it was, because it is a development; it is the climax of things. In Corinthians we have it in germ, but it is fully developed in Ephesians. We cannot get beyond Ephesians.

Ques.   Why is it spoken of as the Spirit of promise here?

C.A.C.   It is important to connect the Spirit with promise; the Spirit comes to us on the principle of promise in contrast to the principle of law. In Galatians 3 there are two principles contrasted, the principle of law and the principle of promise. The apostle takes pains to say that the inheritance is not on the principle of law but on the principle of promise. It is on the principle of what God proposes in His love to give. The Holy Spirit is the Spirit of promise; He is connected with that side of things. He is connected with the things that have their origin in the God and Father of our Lord Jesus Christ.

Acts 1 speaks of the promise of the Father and refers back to all that God said about the Spirit. The Spirit is connected with the Father in a direct way and belongs to the great realm of grace where all things are of the Father.

H.B.   Is the Holy Spirit of promise in view of making those things workable?

C.A.C. I suppose that is the thought of sealing, "Ye have been sealed with the Holy Spirit of promise". It conveys to me that there is something in the saints which corresponds to the mind of God. It is very important that we should see that thought in connection with sealing. There must be something there that the Father can approve and commit Himself to, so it is important to see that we are sealed in Christ and not in the flesh.

L.M.   Was the Lord at His baptism in another sphere morally?

C.A.C. The promise of the Father was received by Him when He was exalted to the right hand of God and ascended into the heavens as a glorious Man. It was not Christ after the flesh but Christ ascended to the heavens. He received the Spirit thus and it is after that pattern that we receive Him. The promise of the Father in connection with the Spirit is entirely outside man after the flesh, so those who are sealed are persons who have trusted in Christ. You have finished with yourself; trusting in Christ means that you have passed over to another Man who is at the right hand of God. That is the gospel! There is a glorious Man in heaven who can be trusted, and if we trust in Him there is something that the God and Father of our Lord Jesus Christ can seal.

It is said first that we have trusted in Christ and then that we have believed; the believing is connected with the word of truth. We have pre-trusted in Christ - we have trusted in Him before His display - we Gentiles have pre-trusted in Him. The word of the truth speaks of a risen, exalted and glorified Man. When Christ becomes the trust and substance of the soul God can seal that. There is in the soul of the believer that which is delightful to God. God looks at what I believe and He seals me, not because of anything in myself but because of the excellence of what I believe. What wonderful value there is to God in a heart that has trusted Christ and believed the word of the truth; He cannot withhold the Spirit of promise from that one. It so commends itself to God that He seals it.

L.M.   It is believers who are sealed?

C.A.C.   Yes. We talk of a full gospel and

I have not much confidence in an empty one! but the full gospel is brought out in Ephesians 2. The gospel of your salvation would be the Ephesian gospel; it is salvation which puts you in the heavenlies in Christ and that is a full gospel.

L.M. It takes us beyond Egypt or the wilderness or even Gilgal.

C.A.C. Yes. No one is sealed until he is in Christ. God does not and could not seal anyone in Adam but as we have come to be in Christ God can seal us.

H.B. Ephesians speaks of the truth as it is in Jesus.

C.A.C. Yes, when that is in the heart there is something that God can seal. We now have to do with the testimony of His Son and he that has received His testimony has set to his seal that God is true. We have to put our seal to the truth of God first and then God seals us. He that receives His testimony has set to his seal that God is true; God can be trusted absolutely and no one is sealed until he comes to that. I can trust God absolutely in all that He has said to me; I am certain that God is true although I may not understand it. When you once put your seal you can never reverse it. There is something there that is of value and delightful to God and now He can seal you with His Spirit.

The world makes God a liar and here is a poor outcast who sets to his seal that God is true and God is delighted and He seals Him with His Spirit. This brings us to the realm of divine realities. It is important to see that we are in Christ by the work of God and thus He can seal us with the Holy Spirit of promise. He seals what has value; God does not put His seal on something worthless. It is through the work of God in our souls that we trust in Christ; no man in the flesh would trust in Him.

L.M.   There are very few believers in Christendom who see that there is no good in man.

C.A.C.   I believe there are a vast number who have faith in Jesus as the Saviour who died for them, but they do not see Christ before the face of God for His delight and there is no delight for God outside that Man. If I have gone through Romans 7, I trust in that Man and delight in Him and that delights God and He seals me with the Holy Spirit of promise.

H.B.   Is the Spirit here the earnest of the acquired possession?

C.A.C.   It looks on to the full result for the blessed God in glory. Suppose I have for five minutes a sense of the blessedness of what is going to be secured for God, that is the earnest of the Spirit. The Spirit gives us a sense of the whole realm of glory; He can give it to us for two minutes or for five minutes.

H.B.   What is the earnest?

C.A.C.   It is a bit of the real thing. If I buy a house for a certain sum, I pay a deposit; it is the earnest, part of the full payment. So the Spirit is a substantial part of the scene of glory in our hearts now. We have come here tonight to get enriched in this.

H.B.   The thought here of the Spirit is that we may realise the possibilities.

C.A.C.   It helps to see that this which is said of the Spirit is an utterance of worship; it is not simply doctrine but worship. If we do not worship God in connection with the sealing of the Spirit we have not got much good from it. This is an utterance of worship; things are put before us as a model of how we should speak to God the Father. Our worship is to be on this line; this is the proper line of the worship of the assembly. Abraham built an altar to God who appeared to him; it is how God has appeared to me that gives character to my worship. We do not get sufficiently familiar with the high level; we are more on the low level. The Lord says at the end of Luke, "the promise of my Father"; that is a lower level. The low level of worship is grace. The whole of Luke is really the unfolding of "I ought to be occupied in my Father's business". The dealing with sin, the great supper, the younger son being received into the house, and so on, were all connected with His Father's business. That is the low level, how grace comes out to poor sinners here. The high level is the taking of the subjects of His grace to heaven in the heavenly Man. How He meets us as dead in sins is the low level, but we must not forget that that is not all, there is the high level.

L.M.   A habitation of God in the Spirit?

C.A.C.   That is the low level; it is down here in the sphere of responsibility that God dwells in His people.

L.M.   What about access by one Spirit to the Father?

C.A.C.   Ah! that is the high level! Access by the Spirit is not simply that you have a right to go but that you go. Many feel that they have boldness to go into the holiest who never go in. I may have a ticket to a show but it is no use to me unless I go.

L.M.   Do we go in individually first?

C.A.C.   When you touch it individually you have the consciousness that you are not by yourself; it is the privilege of the whole company, the assembly. We used to be told that we could not say 'Father' individually, but the Lord tells us differently.

L.M.   Is access to the holiest into the presence of God the high level?

C.A.C.   There are three steps in approach to God: (1) On Peter's line, to offer up sacrifices acceptable to God; you offer there at the altar; you are not inside; (2) In Hebrews you draw nigh to God in liberty to enter the holiest, so you are inside, yet it is to God, not the Father; questions of holiness and righteousness are settled so we come to God without fear; (3) In John's gospel you have access to the Father, that is further still: "No one comes to the Father unless by me" (John 14:6) and the Lord speaks of "My Father and your Father". All these enter into the worship of the assembly but we cannot cover all the ground at any one meeting. Perhaps at one time we are more on the line of spiritual sacrifices, that is more the Supper; the holiest is where you have liberty to go as in the love of the new covenant, but we may go that far and not have access to the Father. In that we all move by one Spirit, what a unifying effect that would have! If all were merged in one Spirit we should move together most beautifully. As we get on to these lines we learn more and more the reality of the Spirit as the power to bring us into the greatest nearness to the Father.

L.M.   Is all this before the development of the mystery?

C.A.C.   Quite so. God is dwelling here; that is a permanent thing. Access to the Father is not always enjoyed; we are not always having access. God dwells by the Spirit in a Gentile company so that His character may be known to the world by those in whom He dwells. So all our ways and demeanour are to be expressive of God dwelling in His people. We are privileged to worship God as well as the Father. 'God' is a more comprehensive title; 'Father' stands connected with the economy of grace.

L.M.   God has secured His eternal habitation at the present time.

C.A.C.   His tabernacle will be with men eternally. It is particularly said of the Gentiles that they are builded together by the Spirit. God dwells by the Spirit; it is a spiritual character of things and should affect us in all our ways. God dwells in us by the Spirit. We are never out of it. When the temple was built Solomon asked Jehovah that there might be a testimony going out from that centre. Heaven was God's dwelling but the temple was like an extension of heaven. The house of God is like that. Solomon prayed that strangers should hear of the great Name and the glorious things done in this house. Such testimony is to go out that people should see some representation of God in us. I heard of a man and his wife who were converted by seeing two sisters pass their house on the way to the meetings. They liked their ways and enquired where they went, came to the room, were converted and are now breaking bread. It was their sober demeanour and tranquility on their faces that arrested them.

———————

A Vessel for Christ

Ephesians 5:16-19

A tiny vessel, Lord, to Thee I bring,
A heart that sought from every earthly spring
To gain its longing, but was empty still;
I bring it now to Thee, to take and fill.

Thy grace, that measured once the distance deep
Of Calvary's woe, to seek and save Thy sheep,
Has touched this heart, and made it long for Thee,
Thyself its Treasure and its All to be.

Thy glory now at God's right hand above,
Supreme of all in that blest scene of love,
In sonship tells that heart its wondrous place
In Thee accepted by the Father's grace.

Thy fulness, Lord, of light and love divine,
No thought can grasp, or human mind define;
The whole vast scene of glory will display
That fulness in a quickly coming day.

When all things filled by Thee are wholly blest,
And God's deep love eternally shall rest
In that which ever speaks to Him of Thee,
Thy greatness, Lord, the universe shall see.

But ere that day of bliss and joy supreme,
When Thou shalt be of every tongue the theme,
Let this small vessel prove Thy gracious power
To fill and satisfy it every hour.

Thy beauties, Lord, Thy holy, precious worth,
Surpassing far the fairest joys of earth,
Shall then absorb its true and constant love,
Thyself its Object in those scenes above.

And filled with Thee,
        and formed through grace divine,
By all that fills it, hold it, Lord, as Thine;
To be, in joy and peace that knows no fear,
The happy vessel of Thy pleasure here!

C. A. Coates

225